T0152461

William Godwin by Sir Thomas Lawrence, 1795, engraved by
W. Ridley

Romantic Rationalist:
A William Godwin Reader

Edited with an Introduction by
Peter Marshall

Foreword by John P. Clark

Romantic Rationalist: A William Godwin Reader
Copyright © 2017 Peter Marshall
First published by FREEDOM PRESS, London, in 1986, reprinted 1996
Reprinted with new foreword and corrections

ISBN: 978–1–62963–228–5
Library of Congress Control Number: 2016948154

Cover portrait by Clifford Harper
Cover by John Yates / www.stealworks.com
Interior design by briandesign

10 9 8 7 6 5 4 3 2 1

PM Press
PO Box 23912
Oakland, CA 94623
www.pmpress.org

Printed in the USA by the Employee Owners of Thomson-Shore in Dexter, Michigan.
www.thomsonshore.com

For Jonathan Peter, Maria Charlotte, Rose and Theodore

CONTENTS

ACKNOWLEDGEMENTS

I am indebted to Jenny Zobel for reading the introduction. I would also like to express my thanks to Vernon Richards and the Freedom Press Group for enabling this volume to be first published. It is particularly appropriate that it should appear a century and a half after the death of Godwin, and a century after Kropotkin, the first militant anarchist to recognize Godwin's importance, joined the Freedom Press Group.

Gwynedd, Wales, 1 June 1985

For this third edition, I would like to thank warmly John P. Clark for writing a new foreword. I consider his book *The Philosophical Anarchism of William Godwin* to be the best on Godwin's moral and political philosophy. Ramsey Kanaan and Craig O'Hara of PM Press have wisely published this corrected edition. Elizabeth Ashton Hill has carefully read the text again. Mo Moseley kindly scanned the second edition of the Freedom Press book *The Anarchist Writings of William Godwin* and moved the footnotes to the bottom of each page. Laura March has proofread them. Many thanks also to Clifford Harper for his excellent portrait of William Godwin which has been used on the front cover.

Devon, England, Summer Solstice, 2016

EDITOR'S NOTE

This work is intended to provide a handy collection of William Godwin's most incisive and relevant thoughts, together with an assessment of his influence, a biographical sketch and an analysis of his contribution to anarchist theory and practice. It is usual to consider Godwin only as the author of the philosophical treatise *Enquiry concerning Political Justice* (1793) and the novel *Caleb Williams* (1794) but he was a prolific writer and published more than fifty works. Many of these works are still worth reading and I have therefore selected passages from a wide range. While his style is clear and eloquent, it can be a little ponderous at times and he did not always know when to stop. The present arrangement is therefore generally more consistent than in the originals. The selections are not intended however as a substitute but as an arrow to the works themselves. Although in the linguistic habit of his day, Godwin speaks of 'man', he uses the term to refer to the whole human species, regardless of race or sex.

My own interest in Godwin began in 1971 when I discovered in a dusty second-hand bookshop in the Lanes in Brighton a copy of George Woodcock's biographical study *William Godwin* (1946). It had printed on the inside page: 'Lourdes Convent, Withdean, Brighton'. What terror the good nuns must have felt to have found in their midst the presence of an anarchist, an atheist and an advocate of free love!

In recent years new hardback and paperback editions of *Political Justice* and several full-length studies of Godwin have revived his reputation, but he still remains largely the property of intellectuals and within the confines of academe. Without trivializing the analysis, it is hoped that the present volume will enable Godwin's thought to ferment anew in the libertarian movement.

The text has been corrected throughout and the bibliography brought up to date. Godwin's reputation has rightly increased since the anthology was first published thirty years ago and he deserves to be celebrated as an important philosopher and novelist and his work widely discussed.

Abbreviations of Works by William Godwin

A.S., *An Account of the Seminary* (1783)

Considerations, *Considerations on Lord Grenville's and Mr. Pitt's Bills* (1794)

P.J., *Enquiry concerning Political Justice* (1793; 2nd ed., 1796; 3rd ed., 1798)

Thoughts, *Thoughts Occasioned by the Perusal of Dr. Parr's Spital Sermon* (1801)

T.M., *Thoughts on Man* (1831)

FOREWORD

There is no better way to get a concise but comprehensive introduction to Godwin's political philosophy than to read *Romantic Rationalist: A William Godwin Reader*. The editor, Peter Marshall, has an exhaustive knowledge of Godwin and his works, and it is exhibited well in this collection. Marshall says that the book "is intended to provide a handy collection of William Godwin's most incisive and relevant thoughts, together with an assessment of his influence, a biographical sketch, and an analysis of his contribution to anarchist theory and practice." Through its excellent introduction to Godwin's life and thought, and through the aptly chosen selections from his works, it does all of these things and more. Marshall has, by means of this book, along with his Godwin study and his history of anarchism, made a powerful contribution to demonstrating Godwin's rightful place as a major figure in the history of modern political thought.

Godwin's influence on the anarchist tradition is comparable in some way to that of figures like Spinoza or Kant on mainstream Western political thought. These thinkers are important not so much for their direct relation to historical movements and popular ideologies closely related to them, but for their great theoretical contributions to their political traditions. Similarly, Godwin never had a major impact on the historical anarchist movement; but nevertheless, he is theoretically important and certainly deserves careful attention from anyone interested in libertarian political theory. Indeed, he deserves attention from anyone interested in political theory of any kind. For perhaps the most important thing that this book achieves is to show that if Godwin is evaluated on his own merits he is the theoretical equal of figures such as Machiavelli, Hobbes, Locke, Rousseau and Mill. He deserves to be classed among the "greats" of modern political thought.

Marshall has chosen the selections very capably, and they exhibit admirably what is most important in Godwin's thought. Marshall also contributes an excellent introduction to Godwin's life and the most significant aspects of his thought. In this brief preface, I would like to supplement his efforts with a brief assessment of Godwin's greatest contributions to modern political theory (the case for him to be included among the greats) and also to point out some of the most problematic aspect of his thought. In doing this I also pose the question: "If the project of a 'philosophical anarchism' is a valid one, where might it find inspiration and guidance in Godwin's work, and where might it better look elsewhere?"

The first area in which Godwin deserves much greater recognition, and indeed in which neglect for his contributions is almost scandalous, is his place in the tradition of utilitarian ethics. In fact, Godwin created one of the most extensively developed, consistent, and clearly articulated theories in the history of utilitarianism. He begins with basic utilitarian principles, such as that "morality is that system of conduct which is determined by a consideration of the greatest general good," that all conduct should be "made subservient to public utility," and that "the end of virtue is to add to the sum of pleasurable sensation" as calculated through a principle of strict impartiality. (p. 61 below) On the basis of these principles he develops a sophisticated version of act-utilitarianism, and applies it impressively to a variety of social and political issues.

One of these issues is the question of freedom of thought and expression. Godwin merits an important place in the history of political thought for his very early and very powerfully argued utilitarian defense of such freedom. As Peter Marshall states, "it is one of the most convincing in the English language." (p. 32) Godwin anticipated by over half a century most of the arguments for which John Stuart Mill is given universal recognition. Godwin argues that free expression must be defended on the basis of its contribution to general good of society and for its role in the development of the "higher faculties" of the individual. He links its utility to the progressive emergence of truth, arguing that political authority is notoriously fallible, that even generally false opinions can contribute some elements to truth, and that truth loses its meaning when it does not contend with falsehood. He also points out the evils of attempts to suppress dangerous opinions rather than confronting them forthrightly. In short, Godwin was a quite brilliant writer "on liberty," as the excerpts in this collection demonstrate.

Godwin also deserves recognition as a pioneering theorist of the ethics of punishment. Marshall points out that this is part of Godwin's critique of law, which is "one of the most trenchant" in the history of anarchism. (p. 31) He applies his utilitarian analysis to an assessment of a spectrum of possible justifications of punishment. He presents strong arguments for the rejection of punishment for retribution or revenge, and also discredits the idea of punishment for reformation or correction. His arguments concerning punishment for restraint or disablement and punishment for example or deterrence have both strong and weak points, but are an important contribution to the debate. His entire discussion is significant for helping establish the parameters of discourse in this area at a very early date in the history of modern moral philosophy. Furthermore, his entire discussion of such punitive rationales must be assessed within the context of his general critique of codified law as being over-generalized and incapable of coping with the complexities of human beings and of situations in the real world. His critique thus goes more deeply than do many even today.

Godwin's analysis of property and economic inequality is also of much greater historical and theoretical significance than has usually been recognized. As Marshall notes, his "original and profound treatment of property had great influence on the early socialist thinkers." (p. 36) The anarchist tradition has tended to neglect him unduly in this area, much to its own detriment. He presents some of the most cogent and compelling arguments for distribution according to need. He also develops an early version of a labor criterion of distribution, based on an argument that it is the best practical alternative to strictly just distribution according to need. Moreover, he implicitly suggests a concept of economic exploitation. He is quite eloquent in his denunciation of economic inequality, which he indicts for imposing suffering on the poor, creating dependency rather than autonomy, destroying individuality, creating egoistic and morally degrading rather than altruistic and morally edifying values, sowing strife and discord in society, and producing widespread criminal activity.

The area in which Godwin makes the most profound contribution to the history of political theory is in what Marshall calls Godwin's "resounding criticism" (p. 32) of all complex systems of law, and all centralized political authority. For Godwin, government can have a limited degree of utility only if it is reduced to a minimum, and, in view of the evils of coercion and loss of moral autonomy that it necessarily entails, the goal must be to abolish it entirely in the long run. As he phrases it eloquently, "In proportion as weakness and ignorance shall diminish, the basis of government will also decay. This however is an event which ought not to be contemplated with alarm. A catastrophe of this description would be the true euthanasia of government." (p. 85) Godwin is scathing in pointing out the evils of monarchy and aristocracy, but his thought is perhaps most relevant when he warns of the dangers of irresponsible, statist democracy, of all forms of representative government, and of any system of law that becomes opaque and incomprehensible to the citizens, thus subverting their rational judgement. He further applies his utilitarian principles in arguing that law can never override the right of private judgement and that morality itself is annihilated unless each person is allowed to make a good-maximizing decision concerning obedience to any given law.

The other side of Godwin's political critique is his proposal for an alternative to the centralized state and representative government. While his ideas are not as fully developed here, he deserves recognition as an important early theorist of the decentralization of power, direct democracy, and voluntary confederation, ideas that are of great contemporary importance, from Chiapas, to Rojava, and elsewhere. In his view, the best form of government is a decentralized democracy in which decision-making is kept at the most local (district) level. He holds that the main formal political institution should be a local jury in which ordinary citizens take turns deliberating on important matters concerning the persons and property of the local citizens. He warns of the evils of "numerous assemblies" (p. 107) yet proposes a system of confederation in which an assembly of representatives of the districts would convene for making decisions concerning mutual concerns. However he holds that such assemblies should meet as infrequently as possible and intervene as little as possible in the affairs of the local communities. He describes the system as "a confederacy of lesser republics, with a general congress or Amphictyonic council, answering the purpose of a point of co-operation upon extraordinary occasions." (p. 148) His enduring hope is that reformed education and the gradual spread of enlightenment will lead to a consensus on most issues and that juries and assemblies will ultimately mediate rather than coercing in any way.

This points to a final area in which Godwin deserves much greater recognition, that is, as a major figure in the history of progressive and libertarian education. Marshall rightly calls him "one of the great pioneers" (p. 37) in this area, though his name is seldom mentioned in the vast literature of "alternative education" and "radical education" over the past half-century. His view of social change in general focuses on the importance of the gradual spread of enlightened ideas through informal education and discussion. In this he prefigures later anarchist theorists, especially Elisée Reclus, who stressed the importance of both formal and informal educational activities among various evolutionary processes that are a necessary precondition for later revolutionary changes in society. But his major contribution is his very specific ideas about transforming the education of children. He describes the child as "an individual being, with powers of reasoning, with sensations of pleasure and pain, and with principles of morality," and proposes methods of education that are based on "the exercise of reverence and forbearance." (p. 129) The ideas developed in his short pedagogical text, "An Account of the Seminary," deserve to be included in all histories of educational thought.

Despite all these quite impressive contributions to moral, political and social philosophy, Godwin's thought is far from being free of serious problems and limitations. This is true, for example, of his ethics. The problems in this area are those of any utilitarian position that reduces intrinsic good to the happiness, pleasure or satisfaction experienced by individuals (whether human beings or even sentient beings). The fact that he, like Mill, considers both the quantitative and qualitative aspects of this experience does not solve the problem. Putting aside the fact that such a position limits intrinsic value to certain aspects of the experience of human beings, it also reduces a many-sided and complex human good to its hedonic aspects, and an inescapably social and communal good to a mere aggregate of individual satisfactions. Godwin does not, of course, ignore the social dimensions of things, which would be rather difficult for anyone to do. Yet he has no real conception of the common and the common good. Although he discusses one's obligations to others, he always remains on the level of individual acts of benevolence dictated by calculations concerning maximization of social utility for the sum total of all individuals.

The deeper roots of such problems in Godwin's thought are found in his espousal of an atomistic and anti-holistic conception of social reality. He says explicitly that "society is no more than an aggregation of individuals." (p. 83) Yet it is impossible to understand how the good of a community is achieved if one focuses only on states of individuals or value experience of individuals. Social and natural conditions that are systemically value-generating are morally relevant, and these conditions cannot be reduced to aggregates of states of individuals. Given Godwin's social atomism, he has no grasp of basic anarchist values such as solidarity, mutual aid and co-operation, values that are directly related to such systemic states or communal, rather than merely individual, goods. Indeed, for Godwin, co-operation is a threat to individual autonomy, so that "all supererogatory co-operation is carefully to be avoided, common labour and common meals." (p. 155) He even hopes that automation will eventually eliminate entirely the evil of people working together, so that "the most extensive operations" might eventually be "within the reach of one man." (p. 155)

The other major source of theoretical difficulties is Godwin's one-sidedly rationalistic concept of human knowledge and indeed human nature. He goes so far as to assert that "reason is omnipotent: if my conduct be wrong, a very simple statement, flowing from a clear and comprehensive view, will make it appear to be such." (p. 74) He certainly makes an important point when he observes that the "progress of reason" can lead to a transformation of values and sensibilities. But he vastly underestimates the possibility that, despite a certain degree of progress in knowledge, the contradictions between transformed consciousness and the domination that is sedimented in institutional structures will continue, as will processes of "fetishistic disavowal," and bad faith, in which the public has a growing intellectual awareness of certain truths, but manage to act as if they have no such consciousness.

Godwin's rationalistic outlook is combined with an anti-naturalism that is often troubling. He expresses the rather Promethean view that because of the possession of rationality "man" is "raised above the other inhabitants of the globe of earth" and "the individuals of our race are made the partners of 'gods, and men like gods'," (p. 60) This rationalistic anthropocentrism is combined with a certain disdain for the material world and for nature. Godwin was for a time inclined toward a kind of Platonism and over his life drifted increasingly in the direction of a form of immaterialism. To the extent that he recognizes even the existence of the material world, he goes so far as to praise Benjamin Franklin for his speculation that "mind would one day become omnipotent over matter." (p. 155) And despite certain romantic tendencies in regard to nature in his literary works, and references to "the bounties of nature," he is capable of judging that "the spontaneous productions of the earth are few, and contribute little to wealth, expenditure or splendour." (p. 122) Thus, he is far from giving the intrinsic value and creative powers of nature their due.

A final area in which Godwin's thought leaves something to be desired is his view of social transformation. Marshall is correct in both the positive and negative sides of his assessment when he observes that "while Godwin offers a subtle and compelling vision of a free and equal society, he offers little advice about the way we are to achieve it." (p. 44) Basically, Godwin advises us to work diligently on behalf of education and enlightenment, and then to wait patiently for the effects of these processes gradually to pervade the entire society. "Imperfect institutions," he explains, "cannot long support themselves when they are generally disapproved of, and their effects truly understood. There is a period at which they may be expected to decline and expire almost without an effort." (p. 112) But we know that they can persist for quite a long time, during which an enlightened segment of the population may disapprove, yet is unable to convince the unenlightened and powerful to change their minds. The linear progressive course of history that Godwin relies on is in the end an object of faith, not of reason.

Godwin's political strategy is to rely as much as possible on gradual enlightenment and to minimize individual any use of force (whether through coercive law or violent revolution). He says that "I shall never be justifiable in having recourse to the latter, while there is any rational hope of succeeding by the former." (p. 113) He foresees an end to inequality as the idea of political justice spreads, and the wealthy minority agree to redistribute voluntarily what they have unjustly accumulated at the expense of the majority. Yet this is the system that was the downfall of the Gandhian Sarvodaya Movement when the successful strategy of massive direct action that overthrew Empire was succeeded by the idea of "trusteeship," in which moral persuasion would lead the rich gradually and voluntary to redistribute their wealth, including all the land and means of production.

Still, Godwin himself perhaps supplied the moral rationale for adopting a strategy of direct action. There are, he notes, "cases that supersede the ordinary law of property." (p. 123) He asks concerning such cases, "What shall prevent me from taking by force from my neighbour's store, if the alternative be that I must otherwise perish with hunger? What shall prevent me from supplying the distress of my neighbour from property that, strictly speaking, is not my own, if the emergency be terrible, and will not admit of delay?" (p. 124) But in view of the vast suffering and moral degradation that Godwin shows to be inherent in economic inequality, it can only be judged a protracted emergency that is indeed "terrible." Godwin himself judges that "he then that is born to poverty, may be said, under another name, to be born a slave." (p. 115)

The implications of such ideas must place in question Godwin's extreme gradualism. Since a vast system of slavery (whether capitalism or literal slavery) is nothing other than a massive system of domination and moral degradation, one can hardly argue that the general good is served by relying on the gradual spread of enlightened opinion to slowly change such a system, while multitudes live and die in slavery. Thus, one can imagine a kind of revolutionary direct action ("Left Godwinianism"?) that would, on the basis of Godwin's own presuppositions, go far beyond the philosopher's gradualist predispositions.

Such questions need to be the topic of continual debate in anarchist and libertarian political theory. Such debate can only be enriched by the inclusion of the deepest insights and best arguments found in the thought of William Godwin. For this reason, Peter Marshall once more deserves our thanks for his efforts in making those insights and arguments more readily available to a larger audience.

John P. Clark, New Orleans

INTRODUCTION

I

INFLUENCE

William Godwin, an unassuming ex-minister and political journalist, woke up one day in 1793, to find that he was famous. His *Enquiry concerning Political Justice*, inspired by the explosive experience of the French Revolution and the vigorous political debate which followed in Britain, swept the board. 'He blazed', his fellow radical William Hazlitt wrote later, 'as a sun in the firmament of reputation; no one was more talked of, more looked up to, more sought after, and wherever liberty, truth and justice was the theme, his name was not far off. . . . No work in our time gave such a blow to the philosophical mind of the country as the celebrated *Enquiry concerning Political Justice*.'[1]

William Pitt's government, shaken by the revolutionary ideas sweeping the country and the formation of political associations clamouring for reform, fully realized the danger of Godwin's work, which offered the first clear statement of anarchist principles. Pitt however decided not to prosecute Godwin for treason (which carried the death penalty) on the grounds that 'a three guinea book could never do much harm among those who had not three shillings to spare'.[2] The book in fact was sold at half the price, and while this was still more than half the average monthly wages of a labourer, working people banded together in hundreds of places to buy it by subscription and to read it aloud at their meetings. Pirated editions appeared in Ireland and Scotland; radical publishers issued lengthy extracts in cheap collections. There

---

1 William Hazlitt, "William Godwin," in *The Spirit of the Age; or, Contemporary Portraits* (Oxford: Oxford University Press, 1954), 19–20; originally published in 1825.

2 C. Kegan Paul, *William Godwin: His Friends and Contemporaries*, Vol. I (Boston: Roberts Brothers, 1876), 80.

was sufficient demand for Godwin to revise the work for cheaper editions in 1796 and 1798. It not only influenced artisan leaders like John Thelwall and Francis Place, who were laying the foundations of the British labour movement, but obscure young poets like Wordsworth, Southey and Coleridge. Indeed, Godwin's ideas expressed the aspirations of the emerging working class and dissenting intellectuals to such an extent that a contemporary observed that 'perhaps no work of equal bulk ever had so many proselytes in an equal space of time'.[3]

The very success of Godwin's work, despite its philosophical weight and elegant style, shows how near the Britain of the 1790s was to revolution. The war declared by Pitt on revolutionary France however soon raised the spectre of British patriotism. His systematic persecution of the radical leaders and the introduction of Gagging Acts in 1794 eventually silenced and then broke the reform movement for a generation. Godwin came boldly to the defence of civil liberties and of his radical friends in a series of eloquent pamphlets but by the turn of the century, he too had fallen into one common grave with the cause of liberty. Thrown up by the vortex of the French Revolution, he sank when it subsided. Most people in the ruling class, De Quincey wrote, felt of Godwin with 'the same alienation and horror as of a ghoul, or a bloodless vampyre'.[4]

But not all was lost. It was with 'inconceivable emotions' that the young Percy Bysshe Shelley found in 1812 that Godwin was still alive and he went on not only to elope with his daughter but to become the greatest anarchist poet by putting Godwin's philosophy to verse.[5] Robert Owen, sometimes called the father of British socialism, became friendly soon after and acknowledged Godwin as his political master. In the 1830s and 1840s, at the height of their agitation, the Owenites and Chartists reprinted many extracts from Godwin's works in their journals and brought out a new edition of *Political Justice* in 1842. Through the early British socialist thinkers, especially William Thompson and

---

3   John Fenwick, "Mr. William Godwin," in *Public Characters of 1799–1800* (1799), 374.

4   Thomas de Quincey, *Collected Writings*, Vol. III, ed. David Masson (Edinburgh: Adam and Charles Black, 1897), 25.

5   Frederick L. Jones, ed., "Percy Bysshe Shelley to Godwin, 3 January 1812," in *The Letters of Percy Bysshe Shelley*, Vol. I (Oxford: Oxford University Press, 1964), 220.

Thomas Hodgskin, Godwin's vision of the ultimate withering away of the state and of a free and equal society began to haunt the Marxist imagination.

Yet despite Godwin's influence on the British labour movement, he was virtually lost to the main international anarchist tradition in the nineteenth century. Proudhon, the first self-styled anarchist, only mentions Godwin twice as a communist of the same school as Owen.[6] There is no evidence that Bakunin read him. Tolstoy spoke of Godwin as providing the answer to the question of how society could be established without a state authority, quoted him on law, and shared his views of reason and perfectibility, but he worked out his ideas independently.[7] It was Kropotkin who rediscovered Godwin for the anarchist movement in the twentieth century, recognizing that the author of *Political Justice* was the first person to state 'in a quite definite form the political and economic principles of anarchism'.[8] The anarchist historian Max Nettlau concurred. The sentiment was further echoed by Rudolf Rocker and confirmed by the studies of George Woodcock.[9]

Since the Second World War, complete English editions of *Political Justice* have appeared in Toronto and London, a Spanish translation in Buenos Aires and a French translation in Toronto, and abridged versions in Los Angeles, London, Tokyo, Bombay, Naples and Oxford. In 1953, the Belgian anarchist Hem Day (i.e., Marcel Dieu) devoted the first issue of his *Cahiers de Pensée et Action* to a collection of penetrating and sympathetic essays by an international symposium of anarchists on 'Un Précurseur Trop Oublié'.[10] A host of academic studies and articles have further recognized Godwin as a serious political philosopher, an

---

6   Pierre-Joseph Proudhon, *Système des contradictions économiques ou philosophie de la misère* (Paris: Guillaumin et cie, 1846).

7   Leo Tolstoy, *Complete Works* (Moscow: 1953) XXXV 205–6; XXXVII 222; XLIV 159.

8   Peter Kropotkin, *Modern Science and Anarchism* (1912), 13–14.

9   Max Nettlau, *Bibliographie de l'anarchie*, Vol. 8 (Bruxelles: 1897), 4–5; Rudolf Rocker, *Anarchism and Anarcho-syndicalism* (Secker & Warburg, 1938), 6; George Woodcock, *William Godwin: A Biographical Study* (Montréal: Black Rose Books, 1989), 254, originally published in 1946; "William Godwin," in *Anarchism: A History of Libertarian Ideas and Movements* (Harmondsworth: Penguin Books, 1975), 65.

10 *Cahiers de Pensée et Action* I (Bruxelles, 1953), 1–80.

original moral thinker, a pioneer in communist economics and progressive education and a powerful novelist.

Godwin is no longer a 'neglected prophet of individual freedom'.[11] He is not only the greatest radical British philosopher but the most profound exponent of philosophical anarchism. He is moreover not merely of historical interest. *Political Justice* finds echoes in the 'counter culture' of the sixties and seventies which questions the validity of the modern industrial state and celebrates the values of simplicity and sincerity and the joy of freedom. He speaks directly to the new radicalism which has emerged in the latter half of the twentieth century and at the beginning of the twenty-first century, which seeks a libertarian way between the bureaucratic centralism of socialist states and the organized lovelessness of the capitalist world. The more they fail, the more attractive anarchism appears. As governments East and West grow more authoritarian, secretive and centralized, Godwin's insights are being increasingly appreciated. Never since the time of the French Revolution has his message been so urgent, relevant and interesting.

---

11 Isaac Kramnick, Introduction to *Enquiry concerning Political Justice*, by William Godwin (Harmondsworth: Penguin Books, 1976), 38.

II

THE MAKING OF AN ANARCHIST

Godwin at first sight would appear an unlikely candidate to become the first and greatest philosopher of anarchism. He was born in 1756 in Wisbech, the capital of North Cambridgeshire, at a time when Britain was expanding its empire in America and India and the Industrial Revolution was about to begin. Britain was developing into a powerful nation state, but the landed gentry still controlled power and Parliament was corrupt and dependent on the Crown.

The region of East Anglia in which Godwin grew up had a long tradition of rebellion. The local peasantry and artisans retained something of the staunch independence which had inspired in 1549 the revolt of 20,000 men against enclosures of common land. In the following century, they participated enthusiastically in the English Revolution, helped organize the Independent movement against the king and listened to the teachings of the Levellers. They would also have heard of the Diggers, those proto-anarchists inspired by Gerrard Winstanley who rejected all man-made laws, obeyed only the dictates of reason and tried to farm the land in common.

Godwin moreover was born into a family of Dissenters who rejected the Church of England and its articles of faith. Although officially tolerated since 1689, the Dissenters were unable to have their births registered, to enter the national universities, or to hold public office. The result was that they formed a separate and distinct cultural group and made up a permanent opposition to the State of England. Godwin was steeped in this tradition: his grandfather had been a leading Dissenting minister, his father was a minister and he aspired from an early age to follow in their footsteps.

Godwin was the seventh of thirteen children and was brought up in a tiny village called Guestwick in the northern part of Norfolk. The atmosphere at home was pious and austere; on one occasion, his father even rebuked Godwin for stroking the cat on Sunday. He was however liberal in politics and religion and would sit in his meeting-house in 'Cromwell's chair', so named because it was said to have been a gift from the leader of the English Revolution. While Godwin's father was stern and remote, his mother was simple and affectionate and his subsequent rejection of the ties of family do not seem to have been the result of a particularly unhappy home life. Unlike his brothers and sister, Godwin proved to be an unusually serious boy, both deeply religious and intellectually precocious. It was decided to send him at the age of eleven to become the sole pupil of a reverend Samuel Newton in the great city of Norwich. It was to prove the most formative period of Godwin's life.

Newton was a powerful figure among Norwich Dissenters; he was also a petty tyrant. Godwin recalls that he was 'like a butcher, that has left off trade, but would with transport travel fifty miles for the pleasure of felling an ox'. His wife was an 'animated statue of ice'. Hitherto Godwin had heard only constant praise from those about him; now Newton complained of his proud stubbornness and proceeded to birch him. The idea of such a violation had for Godwin something in it as abrupt as a fall from heaven to earth. It left Godwin with an indelible hatred of corporal punishment in particular and of coercion and tyranny in general.

But while Godwin rebelled against Newton's sadistic rule, he adopted many of his beliefs which were profoundly to shape his future philosophy. Newton was in fact a member of an obscure Calvinist sect that followed the teachings of Robert Sandeman. Sandeman was the most extreme Calvinist in the eighteenth century; Godwin joked sardonically that whereas Calvin had condemned ninety-nine in a hundred to eternal punishment, Sandeman contrived a scheme for damning ninety-nine in a hundred of the followers of Calvin.[1] At the same time, Sandeman lay great stress on reason: grace was to be achieved not by good works or faith, but by the rational perception of truth, the right or wrong judgement of the understanding. The Sandemanians moreover interpreted literally the teachings of the New Testament to practice brotherly love and share their wealth among the members of their sects.

---

1   Quoted in Peter H. Marshall, *William Godwin* (New Haven: Yale University Press, 1984), 19.

They were also democratic and egalitarian, both rejecting majority rule in favour of consensus and annihilating the distinctions of civil life within the sect. All men and women, they affirmed, are equally fit to be saved or damned.

Godwin went on of course to pull the Calvinist God down from the heavens and to believe in the innocence and perfectibility of all human beings, but he retained much of the social and economic teaching of the Sandemanians. Indeed, he held that morality principally depended on doing to others as we would wish to be done unto, and that property is a trust to be distributed to the most needy.

He not only traced his excessive stoicism and condemnation of the private affections to his early Calvinism, but specifically held Sandemanianism responsible for his central belief that rational judgement is the source of human actions. On leaving Newton's intellectual and emotional hothouse, Godwin entered at the age of seventeen the Dissenting Academy at Hoxton, one of the best centres of higher education in eighteenth-century England. Godwin received here a thorough grounding in Locke's psychology which saw the mind as a blank sheet, in Newtonian science which pictured the universe as a machine governed by natural laws, and in Hutcheson's ethics which upheld benevolence and utility as the cornerstones of virtue. The academy was extremely favourable to free enquiry, and Godwin formed in his own time a belief in determinism, or in the philosophical language of the day, 'necessity' (i.e., all actions are determined), and in idealism or 'immaterialism' (i.e., the external world is created by the mind). These beliefs subsequently underwent no fundamental change.

Godwin's tutors were also extremely liberal in their views. In religion, they denied the divinity of Christ and original sin. In politics, they looked back to the Glorious Revolution of 1688 as the happiest era in British history and were strenuous advocates of the civil rights of humanity.

Godwin was a Tory and a Sandemanian when he entered Hoxton Academy. Being cautious about accepting new ideas and fearful of eternal punishment, he left five years later with his beliefs intact. He was determined as ever to enter the ministry. Three times he tried to become a minister, and three times he was rejected by rural congregations. They no doubt disliked his learned sermons and pricklish manner. His intellectual development during this time however was rapid and the liberal influence of Hoxton Academy had its effect. The political debate raging over the American War of Independence led him to support the Whig opposition to the war, and the reading of Roman historians and Jonathan Swift made him a republican overnight. Then when he was living quietly in Stowmarket as a candidate minister at the age of twenty-six, an artisan put into his hands the works of D'Holbach, Helvétius and Rousseau, the most subversive philosophers of the French Enlightenment whose banned works were causing an uproar on the other side of the Channel.

Godwin read in Rousseau that man is naturally good but corrupted by institutions, that the foundation of private property was the beginning of the downfall of humanity, and that man was born free, and everywhere he is in chains. From Helvétius and D'Holbach, he learned that all men are equal and society should be formed for human happiness. When he closed the covers of their books, his whole world view had changed. They immediately undermined his Calvinist view of man, although for the time being he became a follower of Socinus (who denied the divinity of Christ and original sin) rather than an atheist. Realizing that he was not cut out to be a minister, Godwin decided to go to London and try to earn his living by teaching and writing.

Godwin's first book was the *Life of William Pitt, Earl of Chatham* (1783), which was little more than a meandering biography of the Tory politician. He then wrote a couple of vigorous pamphlets on the Whig side, *A Defence of the Rockingham Party* (1783) and *Instructions to a Statesman* (1784), and a lively and ironic collection of literary imitations, *The Herald of Literature* (1783). These were followed by three short novels written in quick succession, *Damon and Delia* (1784), *Italian Letters* (1784) and *Imogen* (1784), which were useful stylistic experiments and reflected a growing social criticism. Eager to rid himself of his sermons he published a selection in *Sketches of History* (1784), but not without the observation that God acts like a 'political legislator' in a 'theocratic state' and that he has 'not a right to be a tyrant'.[2]

The most important political work of this period was undoubtedly *An Account of the Seminary* (1783), about a school Godwin intended to open in Epsom for the instruction of twelve pupils in the Greek, Latin, French and English languages. Although no pupils turned up,

---

2   William Godwin, *Sketches of History. In Six Sermons* (1784), 20.

the prospectus remains one of the most incisive and eloquent accounts of libertarian and progressive education. It shows Godwin believing that children are not only born innocent and benevolent, but that the tutor should foster their particular talents and treat them gently and kindly. The ex-Tory student and Calvinist minister had moreover come to recognize that:

> The state of society is incontestably artificial; the power of one man over another must be always derived from convention, or from conquest; by nature we are equal. The necessary consequence is, that government must always depend upon the opinion of the governed. Let the most oppressed people under heaven once change their mode of thinking and they are free. . . . Government is very limited in its power of making men either virtuous or happy; it is only in the infancy of society that it can do anything considerable; in its maturity it can only direct a few of our outward actions. But our moral dispositions and character depend very much, perhaps entirely, upon education.[3]

Five years before the French Revolution, Godwin had already worked out the main outlines of *Political Justice*.

Since none of these early works brought Godwin much money, he eagerly accepted an offer to write the political and historical sections of the Whig journals *The New Annual Review* and *The Political Herald, and Review*. Through them, he not only gained a close knowledge of contemporary political affairs but took the opportunity to attack the younger Pitt's 'naked, honest, unplausible despotism' as Prime Minister, to castigate his administration's 'cruelty, tyranny, usurpation and avarice' in India, and to urge the 'Freemen and Citizens' of Ireland not to jeopardise their just claim to independence.[4] In 1787, Godwin also published a *History of the Internal Affairs of the United Provinces* which narrated the principal events of the recent Dutch Revolution during which the cities had attempted to govern themselves by popular councils. The book concluded prophetically two years before the outbreak of the French Revolution that the 'flame of liberty' first excited in America

---

3   *A.S.*, (1783), 2–3.
4   William Godwin, *Uncollected Writings* (1785–1822), ed. J.W. Marke and B.R. Pollin (Gainesville: Scholars' Facsimiles and Reprints, 1968), 32, 61, 52.

had spread and that 'a new republic of the purest kind is about to spring up in Europe'.[5]

Throughout these years in Grub Street, Godwin lived a lonely and uncertain life. Many a time he was unable to eat his dinner without first carrying his watch or his books to the pawnbroker. He was obliged frequently to change one small lodging for another. But he gradually began to move in radical Dissenting and literary circles. He met Thomas Holcroft, a radical playwright, who became his closest friend, persuaded him to become an atheist and showed him the evils of government and marriage. In 1788, Godwin was present at the Revolution Society, which celebrated the centenary of the Glorious Revolution with toasts which began with 'The Majesty of the People!' and ended with 'May Truth and Liberty prevail throughout the World!'

When the French Revolution broke out in the following year, it was not therefore entirely unexpected. Godwin was thirty-three at the time, and, no less than William Blake and Wordsworth, his 'heart beat high with great swelling sentiments of Liberty'.[6] He did not remain idle. When Thomas Paine's publisher faltered, Godwin helped bring out the first part of the *Rights of Man* (1791) and was no doubt impressed by the claim in the second part that 'the more perfect civilization is, the less occasion has it for government'.[7] He also wrote a letter at this time to the Whig politician Sheridan declaring that 'Liberty leaves nothing to be admired but talents and virtue . . . give a state but liberty enough, and it is impossible that vice should exist in it.'[8] As his daughter Mary later observed, Godwin's belief that 'no vice could exist with perfect freedom' was 'the very basis of his system, the very keystone of the arch of justice, by which he desired to knit together the whole human family'.[9]

Burke's reactionary *Reflections on the Revolution in France* (1791) had triggered off a pamphlet war, but Godwin decided to rise above the controversies of the day and write a work which would place 'the principles

---

5   William Godwin, *History of the Internal Affairs of the United Provinces* (1787), 345.

6   C. Kegan Paul, *William Godwin: His Friends and Contemporaries*, Vol. I (Boston: Roberts Brothers, 1876), 61.

7   Thomas Paine, *The Rights of Man* (1791–2), ed. H. Collins (Harmondsworth: Penguin Books, 1976), 65.

8   Marshall, *William Godwin*, 81.

9   Ibid.

of politics on an immoveable basis'.[10] As a philosopher, he wanted to treat universal principles, not practical details. He therefore tried to condense and develop whatever was best and most liberal in political theory. He carefully marshalled his arguments and wrote in a clear and precise style. The result was *An Enquiry concerning Political Justice, and its Influence on General Virtue and Happiness* (1793).

As Godwin observed in his preface, the work took on a life of its own, and as his enquiries advanced his ideas became more 'perspicuous and digested'. He developed a theory of justice which took the production of the greatest sum of happiness as its goal and went on to reject domestic affections, gratitude, promises, patriotism, positive rights and accumulated property. His changing view of government further gave rise to an occasional inaccuracy of language. He did not enter the work, he acknowledged, 'without being aware that government by its very nature counteracts the improvement of individual intellect; but . . . he understood the proposition more completely as he proceeded, and saw more distinctly into the nature of the remedy'.[11] The experience of the French Revolution had already persuaded him of the desirableness of a government of the simplest construction but his bold reasoning led him to realize that humanity could be enlightened and free only with its utter annihilation. Godwin thus set out very close to the English Jacobins like Paine only to finish a convinced and outspoken anarchist— one of great exponents of society without government.

As we have seen, the work had an immediate and tremendous success. Wherever Godwin went, he was received with curiosity and kindness. In the following year appeared his novel *Things as They Are; or, The Adventures of Caleb Williams*, a gripping story of flight and pursuit intended to show how 'the spirit and character of the government intrudes itself into every rank of society'.[12] It too was hailed as a great masterpiece. As well as being praised for its social observation, it has since been recognized as the first thriller and the first psychological novel. A work of Kafkaesque power, it chillingly anticipates the anxieties of modern existentialism.

---

10 Ibid., 82.
11 *P.J.*, (1798) I, viii.
12 William Godwin, *Caleb Williams*, ed. David McCracken (Oxford: Oxford University Press, 1970), 1, originally published 1794.

Godwin's *Political Justice* however could not have appeared at a more untimely moment. It was published a fortnight after Britain declared war on revolutionary France; at a time when the public was 'panic struck' with 'all the prejudices of the human mind in arms against it'.[13] The government decided to try and crush the growing movement which was clamouring for parliamentary reform, by arresting their leaders. When Holcroft was arrested for high treason with Horne Tooke, Thelwall and others, Godwin sprang to their defence at considerable danger to himself by writing some well-argued *Cursory Strictures* (1794) on the charge. He ably showed how the Crown had tried to construct out of many innocent acts a capital crime and to bring a guilty verdict by the 'mere names of Jacobin and Republican'.[14] In the event, a jury threw out the prosecution's case; the influence of Godwin's pamphlet was widely seen as crucial in their decision.

The government would not of course leave it at that. In 1795 there were food riots in the country and meetings of up to 150,000 people took place in London. At the end of October, Londoners thronged the streets shouting 'Down with Pitt! No War! No King!'; a window of the royal coach was even broken as King George III made his way to Parliament. Pitt reacted sharply by introducing his notorious Gagging Acts which abrogated the freedom of speech, assembly and of the press. Godwin again responded by writing some incisive *Considerations on Lord Grenville's and Mr Pitt's Bills, concerning Treasonable and Seditious Practices and Unlawful Assemblies* (1794) and signed them 'By a Lover of Order'. The pamphlet was mainly an uncompromising denunciation of Pitt's policy of repression but Godwin also took the opportunity to criticize the methods of the new political associations, particularly in the London Corresponding Society, for simmering the 'Cauldron of civil contention' through lectures and mass demonstrations.[15] Although Godwin was as vigorous as ever in defending the hard-won liberties of his compatriots, he believed that reform was best achieved through the gradual enlightenment of humanity by discussion and publication in small independent circles. While this has proved one of the chief forms

---

13 *P.J.*, (1798) I, xii.
14 Godwin, *Uncollected Writings*, 158.
15 Ibid., 215.

of anarchist organization, it led at the time to a split between Godwin and the Jacobin agitators like Thelwall.

In the meantime, Godwin's personal life took an unexpected turn. He had long appeared, as Hazlitt put it, like a 'Metaphysician engrafted on the Dissenting Minister' and although he enjoyed the company of women, he was far from being a libertine.[16] In 1796 however he became intimate with Mary Wollstonecraft, the first major feminist writer, who had asserted in her celebrated *Vindication of the Rights of Woman* (1792) that mind has no sex and that women should become rational and independent beings rather than passive and indolent mistresses. Godwin was introverted and diffident, somewhat pedantic, occasionally stubborn and often ill-at-ease in society. Wollstonecraft was bold, passionate and widely experienced. She nevertheless recognized in Godwin an independent spirit who was capable of deep emotion as well as high thinking. They soon became lovers but, aware of the dangers to creativity of cohabitation, lived apart.

Wollstonecraft had an illegitimate daughter by a previous relationship and had experienced the full force of prejudice in the rigid society of the late eighteenth century. She had already tried to commit suicide twice. When she became pregnant again with Godwin's child, she felt unable to face further ostracism and asked Godwin to marry her. Although Godwin had condemned the European institution of marriage as the 'most odious of all monopolies', he agreed.[17] His enemies were delighted by this apparent contradiction between his theory and practice, and the accusation that he had a hot head and cold feet has reverberated ever since. Godwin however as a good anarchist believed that there are no moral rules which should not give way to the urgency of particular circumstances. In this case, he submitted to an institution which he continued to wish to see abolished out of regard for the happiness of the individual. He held himself bound no more than he was before the ceremony had taken place.

Although governmental terror was the order of the day, Godwin still believed that truth would eventually triumph over error and prejudice. He therefore revised carefully *Political Justice*, a new edition of

---

16 William Hazlitt, "William Godwin," in *The Spirit of the Age; or, Contemporary Portraits* (Oxford: Oxford University Press, 1954), 37.

17 See p. 77 in this volume.

which appeared in 1796. Wollstonecraft had helped him recognize the importance of his feelings as a source of human action in his psychology and the central place of pleasure in his ethics. Godwin also made his arguments more consistent by showing from the beginning of the work the evils of government and by clarifying the section of property. Kropotkin was therefore wrong to follow De Quincey in thinking that Godwin had retracted many of his beliefs in the second edition: it not only retained the great outlines of the first but offered a more substantial and convincing exposition of his anarchism.[18] In the third edition of 1798, he further removed a few of the 'crude and juvenile remarks' and added a 'Summary of Principles'.[19]

While revising the second edition of *Political Justice*, Godwin also wrote some original reflections on education, manners and literature which were published as a collection of essays called *The Enquirer* (1797). The work contains some of the most remarkable and advanced ideas on education ever written. Godwin not only argues that the aim of education should be to generate happiness and to develop a critical and independent mind, but suggests that the whole scheme of authoritarian teaching could be done away with to allow children to learn through desire at their own pace and in their own way. His thoughts on economics are no less challenging and incisive. Indeed, the essay 'Of Avarice and Profusion' offered such a trenchant account of exploitation based on the labour theory of value that it inspired Malthus to write his obstacle to all improvement, the *Essay on the Principle of Population* (1798). Godwin's devastating survey 'Of Trades and Professions' in a capitalist society also led the Chartists to reprint it in 1842 at the height of their agitation.

The period spent with Wollstonecraft was the happiest in Godwin's life: it was a union of two great radical minds. Through them the struggles for men's freedom and women's freedom were united at the source. But it was to be tragically short-lived: Wollstonecraft died in giving birth to their daughter Mary. Godwin consoled himself by editing her papers and by writing a moving and frank memoir of her life which was predictably dismissed by the Anti-Jacobins as 'a convenient Manual of

---

18 De Quincey, *Collected Writings*, Vol. XI, 328; Peter Kropotkin, *Ethics: Origin and Development* (New York: Dial Press, 1924), 234n; cf. Woodcock, *Anarchism*, 85.
19 *P.J.*, (1798), xviii.

speculative debauchery'.[20] Godwin never got over the loss of his first and greatest love. All he could do was to re-create her in his next novel *St. Leon* (1799) which showed the dangers of leading too isolated a life and celebrated the domestic affections.

At the turn of the century, Godwin's hopes were shattered. As the reaction against Jacobinism grew, so his reputation waned. He became the subject of a torrent of scurrilous abuse spat from the pulpit and in the lecture theatre and smeared across pamphlets, novels and verse. One of the better poems entitled *Modern Philosophy and the Godwynian System* admirably captures the general tone:

> Far beyond Nature's bounds, he boldly springs,
> And Man's *perfectibility* he sings;
> Fashions a new Utopia's blest domain
> Uncurst with laws, exempt from Custom's rein,
> Where Reason reckless spurns at love and hate,
> And Justice holds with Apathy her state ..
> Ah' grieve not, Anarchists, if heav'n assign
> A transient hour to visions so divine,
> If Nature reassume her ravish'd right,
> And Godwyn's goddess vanish into night.[21]

Godwin did his best to stem the tide in some calm and eloquent *Thoughts Occasioned by the Perusal of Dr Parr's Spital Sermon* (1801), the apostasy of a former friend. He took the opportunity to clarify his notion of justice by recognizing the claim of the domestic affections. He also refuted his chief opponent Malthus by arguing that moral restraint made vice and misery unnecessary as checks to population. But it was to no avail. Godwin was pilloried, laughed at and then quietly forgotten. Never again in his lifetime was he able to capture the public imagination as he had done before.

Godwin now had two young children to bring up alone and little hope for the future. It was therefore with some relief that he met and married a neighbour called Mary Jane Clairmont. She had already two illegitimate children (a boy and a girl) and bore Godwin a son, thereby increasing the family to seven. Although she proved a competent

---

20 Quoted in Marshall, *William Godwin*, 215.
21 Ibid., 231–32.

companion, there was no great passion or intellectual inspiration between the two. Her irritability moreover tested Godwin's immeasurable patience and drove away many of his close friends like Charles Lamb and Coleridge.

With more mouths to feed, Godwin began to write in earnest again. He first turned to writing a play, but it proved a disaster when performed. He then completed a mammoth and well-researched *Life of Chaucer* in 1803 and a new novel *Fleetwood* in 1805. The latter was not only critical of the 'New Man of Feeling' who fails to come to terms with a cruel and barren world, but gave a powerful description of the horrors of child labour in the new factory system. While the characters in his novels look for salvation in small circles in harmony with nature, Godwin was fully aware of the consequences of the Industrial Revolution.

These works brought little fame and less money and on the suggestion of Mary Jane, Godwin decided to set up a publishing firm of children's books called the Juvenile Library. For the next twenty years, it involved him in endless worry and financial complications; he tottered forever on the brink of bankruptcy. But through his many children's histories, biographies, fables, grammars and dictionaries he helped shape the minds of generations of children. As a government spy correctly reported, there appeared 'to be a regular system through all his publications to supersede all other elementary books, and to make his Library the resort of Preparatory Schools, that in time the principles of democracy and Theophilanthropy may take place universally'.[22]

Although Godwin had been howled out of the public arena, younger and more fiery spirits took up his message. Poet Percy Bysshe Shelley, who had been expelled from Oxford for writing a pamphlet on atheism and spurned by his wealthy baronet father, burst into Godwin's life in 1812, *Political Justice* in his pocket and visions of the reign of freedom and justice in his head. Godwin was at first delighted with his greatest disciple, although he tried to check his ardour in fomenting revolution in Ireland. His attitude changed to indignation however when Shelley proceeded to elope with his sixteen-year-old daughter Mary (a 'true Wollstonecraft', he acknowledged), according to his own best theories of free love.[23]

---

22 Ibid., 289–90.
23 Ibid., 36.

His stepdaughter Mary Jane (later known as Claire) also joined them and ended up having a child with Byron. Mary eventually married Shelley and went on to write *Frankenstein* (1818) and other powerful novels. Shelley for his part became partially reconciled to Godwin and raised vast loans on his expected inheritance for the philosopher who excelled in speculation as much as he failed in business. But while Godwin has been accused of being a shameless sponger, if not a 'venerable horseleech', in their financial dealings, they were at least in keeping with their common view of property as a trust which should be distributed to the most needy.[24] Godwin happened to be more on the receiving end in this case, but he too gave to those worse off than himself. He always lived in austere simplicity.

Shelley's intellectual debt to Godwin moreover was immense. What the Bible was to Milton, Godwin was to Shelley. The creed of *Political Justice* was transmuted into the magnificent and resounding verse of the greatest revolutionary narrative poems in the English language. Indeed, in *Queen Mab* (1812), *The Revolt of Islam (1818)*, *Prometheus Unbound* (1819) and *Hellas* (1822), Shelley openly professed an anarchist creed and systematically celebrated the Godwinian principles of liberty, equality and universal benevolence. In his *Philosophical Review of Reform* (1820), he further warned against the 'mighty calamity of government', proposed in its place a 'just combination of the elements of social life', and declared like Godwin that poets and philosophers are the 'unacknowledged legislators of the world'.[25] Although Shelley was never an uncritical disciple and was increasingly drawn to Platonism, he remained to the end faithful to the radiant vision of *Political Justice.* If Godwin is the greatest philosopher of anarchism, Shelley is its poet.

After the end of the Napoleonic Wars, the radical movement with its roots in the 1790s emerged with renewed vigour. Mass demonstrations were held calling for parliamentary reform; on one occasion in 1816, a crowd broke into a gunshop opposite Godwin's bookshop in

---

24 Leslie Stephen, ed., "William Godwin," in *Dictionary of National Biography*, Vol. XXII (New York: MacMillan and Co., 1890), 67.

25 Percy Bysshe Shelley, *Shelley's Prose; or, The Trumpet of Prophecy*, ed. D. L. Clark (Albuquerque: University of New Mexico Press, 1954), 237, 252, 240; see also William Godwin, *Life of Chaucer: The Early English Poet*, Vol. I (London: T. Davison for Richard Phillips, 1803), 370.

Skinner Street which eventually led to the hanging of a rioter on the spot. Three years later, there was the infamous Massacre of Peterloo—recorded in one of Shelley's bitterest poems—when government troops hacked into a defenceless crowd.

Godwin, now in his sixties, remained aloof from the popular agitation. His creed, he told a friend, was a short one: 'I am in principle a Republican, but in practice a Whig. But I am a philosopher: that is, a person desirous to become wise, and I aim at this object by reading, by writing, and a little by conversation.'[26] His writing nevertheless was still vigorous and effective. He composed an impressive new novel set in the seventeenth century called *Mandeville* (1817). It not only gave an eloquent restatement of his moral and political principles, but offered an astonishingly modern account of madness. Three years later, he returned in *Of Population* to attack his chief intellectual opponent Malthus, by a powerful critique of his ratios of population growth and food supply and of his philosophical creed which saw all improvement as futile. Although well received, the work was unable to turn the tide of public opinion.

As a result, Godwin increasingly turned back in his imagination to the period of English Revolution in the seventeenth century. In four vast volumes, he narrated *The History of the Commonwealth* (1824–1828). Surprisingly enough, he only gave the briefest mention to Winstanley and the Diggers whose doctrines so closely anticipated his own. On the other hand, he declared that the five years from the abolition of the monarchy to Cromwell's coup d'état challenged any equal period of English history in the glory of its rule. He defended moreover the execution of Charles I on the grounds that natural justice means that it is sometimes right 'to reinvest the community in the entire rights they possessed before particular laws were established'.[27] There comes a point when 'resistance is a virtue'.[28]

Whilst writing his history, Godwin in 1825 at last fell over the brink and became bankrupt. In the event, it proved a liberation. He sold

---

26 Paul, "William Godwin to Lady Caroline Lamb" (February 25, 1819), in *William Godwin*, op. cit., II, 266.
27 William Godwin, *History of the Commonwealth of England: Vol. I The Civil War* (London: H. Colburn, 1824–28), 90.
28 Godwin, *History of the Commonwealth of England: Vol. II To the Death of Charles I*, 333.

off his bookshop and moved to smaller lodgings with Mary Jane and his library. After the drowning of Shelley, his beloved daughter Mary returned from Italy and proved a great consolation. Although it was increasingly difficult to find a publisher, he produced two more novels, *Cloudesley* (1828) and *Deloraine* (1833), which are still worth reading despite their meandering plots and one-dimensional characters. He wrote some desultory *Lives of the Necromancers* (1834), which reflect his life-long interest in magical powers, and some vigorous essays on religion (published posthumously in 1873), which betray his vague theism and attack the doctrines and practices of Christianity.

The most important work of Godwin's old age was his *Thoughts on Man* (1831), a collection of philosophical essays. They show Godwin holding firm to the fundamental principles of *Political Justice*. In his philosophy, he recognizes that our feelings and sensations lead us to believe in free will and the existence of matter, but he remains strictly speaking a 'necessarian', upholding determinism, and an 'immaterialist', believing that mind is all-pervasive.[29] In his politics, he points out to the reformers who were calling for the secret ballot that it is a symbol of slavery rather than liberty. He is still ready to imagine that 'men might subsist very well in cluster and congregated bodies without the coercion of law'.[30] Indeed, *Thoughts on Man* is a sustained celebration of the achievements and possibilities of the 'godlike being' which makes up our species. After a long and difficult life, Godwin's faith in the perfectibility of humanity remained unshaken, and he ends the book in the confident belief that 'human understanding and human virtue will hereafter accomplish such things as the heart of man has never yet been daring enough to conceive'.[31]

Godwin increasingly found it difficult to manage from his writing so when the new Whig Prime Minister Grey offered him a pension at the age of seventy-seven, he reluctantly accepted. His official title was Office Keeper and Yeoman Usher, and he was given lodgings in the New Palace Yard next to the Houses of Parliament. It was the supreme irony of Godwin's complicated life that the first and greatest anarchist thinker should end his days under the roof of one of the fortresses of

---

29 See p. 52 in this volume.
30 Ibid., VII, 2.
31 Ibid., I, 5.

tyranny. But it was not without a final grandiose, if unintended, gesture. In October 1834, a great fire destroyed the old Palace of Westminster. Godwin was in fact responsible for the fire precautions and equipment, but when the fire broke out he was quietly at the theatre. No one thought of accusing the benign old man of succeeding where Guy Fawkes had failed!

Godwin moved to other lodgings, but he continued to receive his pension. He eked out his last days with his aged wife, his curious library and his rich memories, cheered principally by visits from his daughter. He died peacefully in his bed on April 7, 1836. He had just turned eighty. Only a handful of friends attended the funeral. His final request however was to be buried next to his dearest love Mary Wollstonecraft: in death as in life, the union of the first great anarchist and the first great feminist symbolized the common struggle for the complete emancipation of men and women.

III

ANALYSIS

Godwin set out in *Political Justice* to place politics on an immoveable basis. He did not, like Rousseau and Locke, trace the historical origins of society and government, but preferred to examine the philosophical principles on which they depend. He felt political philosophy should proceed like mathematics by argument and demonstration. His method was therefore strictly deductive: he stated certain propositions, developed their inferences, considered objections and drew conclusions. To this end, he tried to make his style as clear and precise as possible, carefully defining his terms. He addressed himself to the calm friend of truth, although this did not prevent an occasional burst of fervent rhetoric livening the lucid and balanced prose.

As the full title of the first edition *An Enquiry concerning Political Justice, and its Influence on General Virtue and Happiness* implies, Godwin was primarily concerned with the relationship between politics and ethics. Indeed, he conceived politics to be strictly speaking a department of ethics. He further based his ethical principles on a particular view of the universe and human nature. Of all anarchist thinkers, Godwin was the most consistent in trying to show the philosophical assumptions on which he based his libertarian conclusions and hopes.

While it is possible, as Godwin himself suggested, to overlook his more 'abstruse speculations' in philosophy, it is impossible to appreciate his moral and political theory without taking them into consideration.[1] His starting-point is a belief in universal determinism: the universe is a machine governed by necessary laws so that in history and in the life

---

Unless otherwise stated, all quotations in the introduction are taken from the Selections portion of this volume.

1   *P.J.*, (1793) I, 284n.

of the individual nothing could have happened otherwise than it did. The regular succession of causes and effects has the advantage of enabling us in many cases to predict what is about to happen and to model our judgements and actions accordingly. At the same time, Godwin admits that we cannot know the exact nature of causality and that any prediction is based on high probabilities and not certainty. While some superficial thinkers have argued that determinism is inconsistent with a philosophy of freedom, Godwin's position is not unlike Kropotkin's scientific determinism although without his evolutionary perspective.

In the philosophical language of the day, Godwin's form of determinism was called 'necessity' and his meditations on the doctrine whilst writing *Political Justice* led him to become an atheist. 'Religion in all its parts', he wrote, is merely 'an accommodation to the prejudices and weaknesses of mankind.'[2] Nevertheless, like most anarchists Godwin believed in a kind of cosmic optimism: just as nature when left to itself pursues a beneficial path, society when least interfered with flourishes and progresses. In his old age when he adopted a kind of vague theism, Godwin spoke of some 'mysterious power' which sustains and gives harmony to the whole of the universe.[3]

Human nature, no less than external nature, is governed by the laws of necessity. Like Locke, Godwin rejects the theory of innate ideas and instincts but asserts that the 'Characters of Men Originate in their External Circumstances' as one of his chapter titles puts it. In this way, the effects of heredity are minimal; we are almost entirely the products of our environment. It follows for Godwin that we have a common nature and share a great and substantial equality. Existing inequalities are therefore entirely the result of social arrangements; there are no natural grounds for slavery or classes.

Godwin also rejects psychological egoism—the theory that we always act from self-interest—by arguing that we are not only capable of benevolence but that benevolent actions bring the greatest pleasure. At birth we are neither virtuous nor vicious: we will be benevolent or

2   Ibid., II, 797.
3   William Godwin, *Essays Never Before Published* (London: G. G. J. and J. Robinson, 1873), 87.

selfish according to our upbringing and education. From this physical equality Godwin deduces moral equality: since we have a common nature we should be treated with equal consideration and what is to be desired for one is desirable for another.

While Godwin argues that human nature is malleable, he believes that it does have certain characteristics. In the first place, we are social beings, and society brings out our best abilities and sympathies. But Godwin also believes that we are individuals, and that to be truly happy we must not forfeit our individuality by losing ourselves in the mass or by becoming dependent on others.

Secondly, we are rational human beings, capable of recognizing the truth and acting accordingly. We are not merely passive bundles of matter in motion, since it is a fact of experience that mind influences what we call matter and *vice versa*. In the great chain of causes and effects, mind is a real cause and indispensable link. Because human beings have a mind they are also voluntary beings, that is to say, capable of consciously directing their actions.

Looking at human behaviour, Godwin distinguishes between two classes of actions: voluntary and involuntary. Involuntary actions take place without foresight on our part, like when we burst into tears. Voluntary actions on the other hand are the result of conscious motives and occur with an awareness of consequences, like when we decide to resist tyranny or distribute our wealth. As Godwin puts it succinctly in a chapter title: 'The Voluntary Actions of Men Originate in their Opinions'. The most desirable state for Godwin is to widen as far as possible the scope of our voluntary actions and to distance ourselves from the state of mere inanimate machines, acted upon by unknown causes.

It is through reason that Godwin reconciles his philosophy of necessity and human choice. While every action is determined by a motive, reason enables us to choose what motive to act upon. In fact, rather than making moral choices impossible, the believer in necessity employs real causes and can expect real effects: moral approval or disapproval can thus influence conduct. In his later writings, Godwin saw the advantage of believing in a 'delusive sense of liberty' in that it inspired moral energy, but in theory he refused to accept the notion of free will as some mysterious power within us which acted independently of motives.[4]

---

4   Godwin, *T.M.* (1831), 231.

The third chief characteristic of our species for Godwin is that we are progressive beings. Godwin based his notion of the 'perfectibility of man' on the assumptions that our voluntary actions originate in our opinions and that it is the nature of immutable truth to triumph over error. Godwin made the following propositions: 'Sound reasoning and truth, when adequately communicated, must always be victorious over error: Sound reasoning and truth are capable of being so communicated: Truth is omnipotent: The vices and moral weaknesses of man are not invincible: Man is perfectible, or in other words susceptible of perpetual improvement.' Since vice is nothing more than ignorance and opinions necessarily determine actions, education and enlightenment will suffice to make us free, virtuous and wise. Thus we may be products of our circumstances, but we can also change them: we are to a considerable degree the creators of our own destiny.

Several objections have been raised to Godwin's view of the perfectibility of man, but they usually overlook his own clarifications. In the first place, by perfectibility he did not mean that human beings are capable of reaching perfection but rather that they can improve themselves indefinitely. Indeed, he was well aware of the power of evil, the disrupting force of passion and the weight of institutions. Progress, he stressed, will be gradual, often interrupted, and may even have to pass through certain necessary stages.

Secondly, it is sometimes claimed that there is no immutable and universal truth and that truth does not always triumph over error. Although Godwin talked of immutable truths in a Platonic way, he made clear that he did not mean absolute truth but 'greater or less probability'.[5] He was moreover fully informed of the fragility of truth and the strength of prejudice and habit. Nevertheless, it is accurate to say that Godwin believed like John Stuart Mill that truth can fight its own battles and put error to rout. On this reasonable assumption, he developed one of the most powerful defences of the freedom of thought and expression.

Thirdly, it has been argued that people do not always do what they think is right and that Godwin's account of human behaviour is too rational. Clearly, on some occasions there is a gap between thought and action, but it is quite plausible to say that we cannot be really convinced

---

5   *P.J.*, (1796), I, 55n.

of the desirableness of an object without desiring it. As for the accusation of excessive rationality, it is true that Godwin believes that an action can flow from the rational perception of truth and as such the will can be called the last act of the understanding. At the same time, Godwin claimed that 'passion is inseparable from reason', and that virtue cannot be 'strenuously espoused' until it is 'ardently loved'.[6] Godwin further maintained that reason is not an independent principle and in a practical view merely 'a comparison and balancing of different feelings'. But although reason cannot excite us to action, it is calculated to regulate our conduct and it is to reason that we are to look for the improvement of our social condition. It is a subtle view which cannot easily be dismissed.

From these substantial assumptions about human nature, Godwin developed his system of ethics. He was a thoroughgoing and consistent utilitarian, defining morality as that 'system of conduct which is determined by a consideration of the greatest general good'. He is however an act-utilitarian rather than a rule-utilitarian. While he recognizes that general moral rules are sometimes psychologically and practically necessary, he warns against too rigid an application of them. Since no actions are the same, there can be no clearer maxim than 'Every case is a rule to itself.' It is therefore the duty of the just person to contemplate all the circumstances of the individual case in the light of the sole criterion of utility. While it is generally wrong, for instance, to tell lies, it might be right to do so to save my life from instant destruction. Such reasoning not only made Godwin an act-utilitarian but also led him to become the first great anarchist thinker who rejects all rules and laws except the dictates of the understanding.

In his definition of good, Godwin is a hedonist: 'Pleasure and pain, happiness and misery constitute the whole ultimate subject of moral enquiry.' Even liberty, knowledge and virtue are not for Godwin ends in themselves but means in order to achieve happiness. But while he equates happiness with pleasure, some pleasures are undoubtedly better than others. Intellectual and moral pleasures are to be preferred to the physical; indeed, Godwin dismissed sexual pleasure as a 'very trivial object'.[7] The highest form of pleasure is enjoyed by the person of benevolence who rejoices in the good of the whole. But Godwin did not

---

6   Ibid., (1798) I, 81.
7   *P.J.*, (1793), II 851.

think that the higher pleasures should exclude the lower, and he made clear that the most desirable state is that in which we have access to all these sources of pleasure and are 'in possession of the happiness the most varied and uninterrupted'.

As a utilitarian, Godwin defines justice as 'coincident with utility' and infers that 'I am bound to employ my talents, my understanding, my strength and my time for the production of the greatest quantity of general good.' Combined with the principle of impartiality, which arises from the fundamental equality of human beings and is the regulator of virtue, Godwin's view of utility led him to some novel conclusions. While all human beings are entitled to equal consideration, it does not follow that they should be treated the same. When it comes to distributing justice I should put myself in the place of an impartial spectator and discriminate in favour of the most worthy, that is, those who have the greatest capacity to contribute to the general good. Thus in a fire, if I am faced with the inescapable choice of saving either a philosopher or a servant, I should choose the philosopher—even if I were the servant. If the servant had been my brother, my father, my sister, my mother or my benefactor, the case would be the same. 'What magic', Godwin asks, 'is there in the pronoun "my" that should justify us in overturning the decisions of impartial truth?'

Godwin concluded that sentiments like gratitude, friendship, domestic and private affections which might interfere with our duty as impartial spectators have no place in justice. It might be more practical for me to prefer my friends and relatives, but it does not make them more worthy of my attention. Godwin later recognized the importance of the private and domestic affections in developing sympathetic feelings and apprehended them to be 'inseparable from the nature of man, and from what might be styled the culture of the heart'. But while charity might begin at home, he always insisted that it should not end there and that we should always be guided by considerations of the general good.

Godwin's strict application of the principle of utility led him to an original treatment of duty and rights. 'Duty' he defined as 'the treatment I am bound to bestow upon others'; it is that mode of action on the part of the individual which constitutes 'the best possible application of his capacity to the general benefit'. In order for an action to be truly virtuous however it must proceed from benevolent intentions and have long-term beneficial consequences. This duty to practise virtue has serious implications for rights.

While the American and French Revolutions had enshrined lists of rights and Thomas Paine was advocating the *Rights of Man* and Mary Wollstonecraft the *Rights of Woman*, Godwin on utilitarian grounds argued that we have no inalienable rights. Our property, our life and our liberty are trusts which we hold on behalf of mankind, and in certain circumstances justice may require us to forfeit them for the greater good. But while Godwin held that any active or positive right to do as we please is untenable, he did allow two rights in a negative and passive sense. The most important is the right to private judgement, that is a certain 'sphere of discretion' which I have a right to expect shall not be infringed by my neighbour. Godwin also acknowledged the right each man possesses to the assistance of his neighbour. Thus while I am entitled to the produce of my labour on the basis of the right of private judgement, my neighbour has a right to my assistance if he is in need and I have a duty to help him. These rights however are always passive and derive their force not from any notion of natural right but from the principle of utility: they may be superseded whenever more good will result from their infringement than their observance.

Godwin's defence of the right of private judgement is central to his scheme of rational progress and leads him to reject all forms of coercion. As people become more rational and enlightened, they will be more capable of governing themselves, thereby making external institutions increasingly obsolete. But this can only happen if they freely recognize truth and act upon it. Coercion must therefore generally be wrong: it cannot convince but only alienates the mind. Indeed, it is inevitably a 'tacit confession of imbecility'. The person who uses coercion pretends to punish me because his argument is strong, but in reality it can only be because it is weak and inadequate. Truth alone carries its own force. This belief forms the cornerstone of Godwin's criticism of government and law.

On similar grounds, Godwin objects to the view that promises form the foundation of morality. Promises in themselves do not carry any moral weight for they are based on a prior obligation to do justice: I should do something right not because I promised, but because it is right to do it. In all cases, I ought to be guided by the intrinsic merit of the case and not by any other external considerations. A promise in the sense of a declaration of intent is relatively harmless; a promise may even in some circumstances be a necessary evil; but we should make as few of them as possible. 'It is impossible to imagine', Godwin declares, 'a principle of more vicious tendency, than that which shall teach me to disarm future wisdom by past folly . . .' It follows that all binding oaths and contracts are immoral.

Given Godwin's concern with the independent progress of the mind and rejection of promises, it comes as no surprise that he should condemn the European institution of marriage. In the first place, the cohabitation it involves subjects its participants to some inevitable portion of thwarting, bickering and unhappiness. Secondly, the marriage contract can lead to an eternal vow of attachment after a few meetings in circumstances full of delusion. As a law, marriage is therefore the worst of laws; as an affair of property, the worst of all properties. Above all, 'so long as I seek to engross one woman to myself, and to prohibit my neighbour from proving his superior desert and reaping the fruits of it, I am guilty of the most odious of all monopolies'. The abolition of marriage, Godwin believed, would be attended with no evils although in an enlightened society he suggested that relationships might be in some degree permanent rather than promiscuous.

Politics for Godwin is an extension of ethics and must be firmly based on its principles. Since these principles are universal, he felt it was possible to deduce from them the 'one best mode of social existence'.[8] Hence the enquiry into 'political justice'. The term however is somewhat misleading since Godwin does not believe that justice is political in the traditional sense but social: his idea of a perfectly just society would determine how to do away with all government. His overriding aim was to create a society which was free yet ordered; which established 'Liberty without Licentiousness'. His bold reasoning led him to conclude that ultimately order could only be achieved in anarchy.

Like all anarchists, Godwin distinguishes carefully between society and government. With Kropotkin, he argues that human beings associated at first for the sake of 'mutual assistance'. With Paine, he believes that society is in every state a blessing. Man by nature is a social being

---

8   Ibid., I, 237.

and without society he cannot reach his full stature. But society does not create a corporate identity, or even a general will, but remains nothing more than an 'aggregation of individuals'.

It was the 'errors and perverseness of the few' who interfered with the peaceful and productive activities of people which made the restraint of government apparently necessary. But while government was intended to suppress injustice, its effect has been to embody and perpetuate it. By concentrating the force of the community, it gives occasion to 'wild projects of calamity, to oppression, despotism, war and conquest'. With the further division of society into rich and poor, the rich have become the 'legislators of the state' and are perpetually reducing oppression into a system. Government moreover by its very nature checks the improvement of the mind and makes permanent our errors. Indeed, government and society are mutually opposed principles: the one is in perpetual stasis while the other is in constant flux. Since government even in its best state is an evil, it follows that we should have as little of it as the general peace of society will allow. In the long run however Godwin concludes that the 'brute engine' of political government has been 'the only perennial cause of the vices of mankind' and has 'mischiefs of various sorts incorporated with its substance', which are 'no otherwise removable than by its utter annihilation!'

Not surprisingly, Godwin rejects the idea that the justification for government can be found in some original social contract which people decided to set up. Even if there had been a contract, it could not be binding on subsequent generations and in changed conditions. Equally, the idea of tacit consent would make any existing government, however tyrannical, legitimate. As for direct consent, it is no less absurd since it would mean that government can have no authority over any individual who withholds his or her approval. Constitutions, which mean that people are to be governed by the '*dicta* of their remotest ancestors', are open to similar objections by preventing the progress of political knowledge.

In fact, Godwin asserts that all government is founded in opinion. It is only supported by the confidence placed in its value by the weak and ignorant. But in proportion as they become wiser, so the basis of government will decay. At present it is the mysterious and complicated nature of the social system which has made the mass of humanity the 'dupe of knaves' but 'once annihilate the quackery of government, and the most homebred understanding might be strong enough to detect the artifices of the state juggler that would mislead him'. Godwin therefore looks forward to the 'true euthanasia' of government and the implicit opinion on which it is based and believes that there would necessarily follow 'an unforced concurrence of all in promoting the general welfare'.

Laws no less than governments are inconsistent with the nature of truth and mind. Human beings can do no more than declare the natural law which eternal justice has already established. Legislation in the sense of framing man-made laws in society is therefore neither necessary nor desirable: 'Immutable reason is the true legislator. . . . The functions of society extend, not to the making, but the interpreting of law.' Moreover, if the rules of justice were properly understood, there would be no need for artificial laws in society.

Godwin's criticism of law is one of the most trenchant put forward by anarchists. Where liberals and socialists maintain that law is necessary to protect freedom, Godwin sees them as mutually incompatible principles. All man-made laws are by their very nature arbitrary and oppressive. They are not as their advocates claim, the wisdom of ancestors but rather the 'venal compact' of 'superior tyrants', primarily enacted to defend economic inequality and unjust political power. There is no maxim clearer than this, 'Every case is a rule to itself', and yet like the bed of Procrustes, laws try to reduce the multiple actions of people to one universal standard. Once begun laws inevitably multiply; they become increasingly confusing and ambiguous and encourage their practitioners to be perpetually dishonest and tyrannical. 'Turn me a prey to the wild beasts of the desert', Godwin's hero in his novel *Caleb Williams* exclaims, 'so I be never again the victim of a man dressed in the gore-dripping robes of authority!'

Punishment, which is the inevitable sanction used to enforce the law, is both immoral and ineffective. In the first place, under the system of necessity, there can be no personal responsibility for actions which the law assumes: 'the assassin cannot help the murder he commits, any more than the dagger'. Secondly, coercion cannot convince but rather alienates the mind and is unnecessary if an argument is strong and true. Punishment, or 'the voluntary infliction of evil', is therefore barbaric if used for retribution and useless if used for reformation or example. Godwin concludes that wrongdoers should be restrained only as a temporary expedient and treated with as much kindness and gentleness as possible.

With his rejection of government and laws, Godwin condemns any form of obedience to authority other than 'the dictate of the understanding'. The worst form of obedience for Godwin is not however when we obey out of consideration of a penalty (as for instance when we are threatened by a wild animal) but when we place too much confidence in the superior knowledge of others (even to building a house). Bakunin recognized the latter as the only legitimate form of authority, but Godwin sees it as the most pernicious since it can easily make us dependent, weaken our understanding and encourage us to revere our governors.

Godwin's defence of freedom of thought and expression, which is essential for the development of the understanding and the discovery of truth, is one of the most convincing in the English language. All political superintendence of opinion is harmful, because it prevents intellectual progress, and unnecessary, because truth and virtue are competent to fight their own battles. If I accept a truth on the basis of authority it will appear lifeless, lose its meaning and force, and be irresolutely embraced. If on the other hand a principle is open to attack and is found superior to every objection it can never be so securely established. While no authority is infallible, truth emerges stronger than ever through the clash of opposing opinions. All religious tests, oaths and libel laws are therefore plainly pernicious. Godwin adds however that true toleration not only requires that there should be no laws restraining opinion, but that we should treat each other with forbearance and liberality.

Having established his own political principles, Godwin offered a resounding criticism of existing political practices. In the first place, he completely rejects the idea that society as a whole somehow makes up a moral 'individual' in whose overriding interest certain policies must be pursued. The glory and prosperity of society as a whole, he declares, are 'unintelligible chimeras'. Indeed, patriotism or the love of our country has been used by imposters to render the multitude 'the blind instruments of their crooked designs'.

Of all political systems, monarchy is the worst. By his upbringing and his power, 'every king is a despot in his heart' and an enemy of the human race. Monarchy makes wealth the standard of honour and measures people not according to their merit but their title. As such, it is an absolute imposture which overthrows the natural equality of man. Aristocracy, the outcome of the 'monster' feudalism, is also based on false hereditary distinctions and the unjust distribution of wealth. It converts the vast majority of the people into 'beasts of burden'. Democracy on the other hand is the least pernicious system of government since it treats every person as an equal and encourages reasoning and choice.

Godwin's defence of republican and representative democracy is however essentially negative. Republicanism alone, he argues, is not a remedy that strikes at the root of evil if it leaves government and property untouched. Again, representation may call on the most enlightened part of the nation, but it necessarily means that the majority are unable to participate in decision-making. The practice of voting involved in representation further creates an unnatural uniformity of opinion by limiting debate and reducing complicated disputes to simple formulae which demand assent or dissent. It encourages rhetoric and demagoguery rather than the cool pursuit of truth. The whole debate moreover is wound up by a 'flagrant insult upon all reason and justice', for the casting up of numbers cannot decide on truth.

The secret ballot was for many reformers in Godwin's day one of the principal means of achieving political liberty. Yet Godwin as an anarchist could scarcely conceive of a political institution which was a 'more direct and explicit patronage of vice'. Its secrecy fosters hypocrisy and deceit about our intentions whereas we should be prepared to give reasons for our actions and face the censure of others. The vote by secret ballot is therefore not a symbol of liberty but of slavery. Communication is the essence of liberty; ballot is the 'fruitful parent of ambiguities, equivocations and lies without number'.

A further weakness of representative assemblies is that they create a fictitious unanimity. Nothing, Godwin argues, can more directly contribute to the depravation of the human understanding and character than for a minority to be made to execute the decisions of a majority. A majority for Godwin has no more right to coerce a minority, even a minority of one, than a despot has to coerce a majority. A national assembly further encourages every man to connect himself with some sect or party, while the institution of two houses of assembly merely divides a nation against itself. Real unanimity can only result from a society of perfect freedom.

Godwin is quite clear that political associations and parties are not suitable means to reach that society. While the artisans were organizing themselves into associations in order to put pressure on Parliament for reform, Godwin spelled out the dangers. Members soon learn the shibboleth of party and stop thinking for themselves. Without any pretence of delegation from the community at large, associations seize power for themselves. The arguments against government are equally hostile to them. Truth moreover cannot be acquired in crowded halls and amidst noisy debates but dwells with quiet contemplation.

Having witnessed the French Revolution turn into the Terror, during which argument was replaced by the guillotine, Godwin did not give his wholehearted support to revolution in the sense of a sudden and violent transformation of society. Revolution may be instigated by a horror against tyranny, but it can also be tyrannical in turn, especially if there is an attempt to coerce the people through the threat of punishment. While not opposed on principle to armed struggle—I ought for instance to be ready to resist the 'domestic spoiler' or invading despot with the minimum of force if all else fails—Godwin felt it was the duty of the enlightened person to postpone revolution. Godwin may not have been a complete pacifist, but non-violence was his strategy of liberation.

The proper mode of bringing about change is through the gradual diffusion of truth and knowledge. Godwin thus looks to a revolution in opinions, not on the barricades: 'Persuasion and not force, is the legitimate instrument for influencing the human mind.' The reform Godwin recommends (that 'genial and benignant power'!) is however so gradual that it can hardly be considered to have the nature of an action. Since government is founded in opinion, as people become wiser and realize that it is an unnecessary evil, it will eventually wither away. It follows that the true equalization of society is not to reduce all to a 'naked and savage equality' but to elevate every person to true wisdom. This process cannot of course be realized by parties or political associations: Godwin looks to bold and thoughtful guides who would speak the truth and practise sincerity and thereby act as catalysts of change. They should nevertheless form nothing greater than small and independent circles. In this Godwin sketched the outline of the typical anarchist group which is autonomous and self-directing.

Godwin argued that it is not enough to dissolve government and leave property relations as they are. In this, he departs from the liberal tradition and aligns himself with socialism. Indeed, he considers the subject of property to be the 'key-stone' that completes the fabric of political justice. His economics, like his politics, is an extension of his ethics. The first offence, Godwin argues with Rousseau, was committed by the man who took advantage of the weakness of his neighbours to secure a monopoly of wealth. Since then there has been a close link between property and government for the rich are the 'indirect or direct legislators of the state'. The resulting moral and psychological effects of unequal distribution have been disastrous on both rich and poor alike. Accumulated property creates a 'servile and truckling spirit', makes the acquisition and display of wealth the universal passion, and hinders intellectual development and enjoyment. By encouraging competition, it reduces the whole structure of society to a system of the narrowest selfishness. Property no longer becomes desired for its own sake, but for the distinction and status it confers.

To be born to poverty, Godwin suggests, is to be born a slave; the poor man is 'strangely pent and fettered in his exertions' and becomes the 'bond slave of a thousand vices'. The factory system, with its anxious and monotonous occupations, turns workers into machines and produces a kind of 'stupid and hopeless vacancy' in every face, especially among the children. Painfully aware of the consequences of the Industrial Revolution, Godwin laments that in the new manufacturing towns if the workers managed to live to forty, 'they could not earn bread to their salt'. The great inequalities in European countries can only lead to class war and incite the poor to reduce everything to 'universal chaos'.

In place of existing property relations, Godwin proposes a form of voluntary communism. His starting-point is that since human beings are partakers of a common nature, it follows on the principle of impartial justice that the 'good things of the world are a common stock, upon which one man has as valid a title as another to draw for what he wants'. Justice further obliges every person to regard his or her property as a trust and to consider in what way it might be best employed for the increase of liberty, knowledge and virtue. But justice is reciprocal: every man has a duty to assist his neighbour as well as a claim to his assistance.

Godwin recognizes that money is only the means of exchange to real commodities and no real commodity itself. There is no wealth in the world except the labour of man. What is misnamed wealth is merely 'a power invested in certain individuals by the institution of society, to compel others to labour for their benefit'. Godwin could therefore see no justice in the situation in which one man works, and another man is idle and lives off the fruits of the labour of his fellows. It would be fairer if all worked. Since a small quantity of labour is sufficient to provide the means of subsistence, it would moreover increase the amount of leisure and allow everyone to cultivate his or her understanding and to experience new sources of enjoyment.

Godwin deepens his analysis by distinguishing between four classes of things: the means of subsistence, the means of intellectual and moral improvement, inexpensive pleasures and luxuries. It is the last class that is the chief obstacle to a just distribution of the previous three. From this classification, Godwin deduces three degrees of property rights. The first is 'my permanent right in those things the use of which being attributed to me, a greater sum of benefit or pleasure will result than could have arisen from their being otherwise appropriated'. This includes the first three classes of things. The second degree of property is the empire every person is entitled to over the produce of his or her own industry. This is only a negative right and in a sense a sort of usurpation since justice obliges me to distribute any produce in excess of my entitlement according to the first degree of property. The third degree, which corresponds to the fourth class of things, is the 'faculty of disposing of the produce of another man's industry'. It is entirely devoid of right since all value is created by labour and it directly contradicts the second degree.

Godwin thus condemns capitalist accumulation. On the positive side, he advocates that all able-bodied people should work and that all members of society should have their basic needs satisfied. But just as I have a right to the assistance of my neighbour, he has the right of private judgement. It is his duty to help me satisfy my needs, but it is equally my duty not to violate his sphere of discretion. In this sense, property is founded in the 'sacred and indefeasible right of private judgement'. At the same time Godwin accepts on utilitarian grounds that in exceptional circumstances it might be necessary to take goods by force from my neighbour in order to save myself or others from calamity.

Godwin's original and profound treatment of property had great influence on the early socialist thinkers. He was the first to write systematically about the different claims of human need, production and capital. Marx and Engels acknowledged his contribution to the development of the theory of exploitation and even considered translating *Political Justice*.[9] In the anarchist tradition, he anticipates Proudhon by making a distinction between property and possession. In his scheme of voluntary communism however he comes closest to Kropotkin.

Godwin saw no threat from the growth of population to upset his communist society. Like all anarchists, he rested his hopes in a natural order or harmony: 'There is a principle in the nature of human society by means of which everything seems to tend to its level, and to proceed in the most auspicious way, when least interfered with by the mode of regulation.' In addition, there is no evidence for natural scarcity; much land is still uncultivated and what is cultivated could be improved. And even if population did threaten to get out of hand there are methods of birth control. Malthus of course could not leave it at that and in his *Essay on the Principle of Population* (1798) he argued that population grows faster than the food supply and that vice and misery must therefore remain as necessary checks. But Godwin counterattacked with his doctrine of moral restraint or prudence, questioned the validity of Malthus's evidence, and rightly suggested that people would have fewer children as their living standards improved.

The principal means of reform for Godwin is through education and his original reflections on the subject make him one of the great pioneers of libertarian and progressive education. Godwin, perhaps more than any other thinker, recognizes that freedom is the basis of education and education is the basis of freedom. The ultimate aim of education, he maintains, is to develop individual understanding and to prepare children to create and enjoy a free society.

In keeping with his view of human nature, he believed that education has far greater power than government in shaping our characters. Children are thus a 'sort of raw material put into our hands, a ductile and yielding substance'. Nature never made a 'dunce' and 'genius' is not innate but generated and acquired. It follows that the so-called

9   Karl Marx and Friedrich Engels, *The German Ideology*, ed. C.J. Arthur (New York: International Publishers, 1970), 20; Engels to Marx (March 17, 1845), quoted in Max Nettlau, *Der Vorfrühling der Anarchie* (Berlin: Der Syndikalist/ Fritz Kater, 1925), 73.

vices of youth derive not from nature but from the defects of education. Children are born innocent: confidence, kindness and benevolence constitute their entire temper. They have a deep and natural love of liberty at a time when they are never free from the 'grating interference' of adults. Yet liberty is the 'school of understanding' and the 'parent of strength'; indeed, Godwin suggests that children learn and develop more in their hours of leisure than at school.

For Godwin all education involves some form of despotism and the tyranny of implicit obedience. Modern education not only corrupts the hearts of children, but undermines their reason by its unintelligible jargon. It makes little effort to accommodate their true capacities. National or state education, the great salvation of many progressive reformers, can only make matters worse. Like all public establishments, it involves the idea of permanence and actively fixes the mind in 'exploded errors': the knowledge taught in universities and colleges is way behind that which exists in unshackled members of the community. In addition, it cannot fail to become the mirror and tool of government, forming an alliance more formidable than that of church and state and teaching a veneration of the constitution rather than of truth. In these circumstances, it is not surprising that the teacher is the worst of slaves by being constantly obliged to rehandle the foundations of knowledge; and a tyrant, by forever imposing his will and checking the pleasures and sallies of his charges.

Having analysed the deficiencies of existing modes of education, Godwin admits that education in a group is preferable to solitary tuition in developing talents and encouraging a sense of personal identity. In existing society, a small and independent school is probably the best. But Godwin goes further to question the very foundations of traditional schemes of education.

The aim of education, he maintains, must be to generate happiness. Since virtue is essential to happiness, and to make a person virtuous he or she must become wise, education should develop a mind which is 'well-regulated, active and prepared to learn'. This is best achieved not by inculcating in young children any particular knowledge but by encouraging their latent talents, awakening their minds and forming clear habits of thinking.

In our treatment of children, we should be egalitarian, sympathetic, sincere, truthful and straightforward. We should not become harsh monitors and killjoys; the extravagances of youth are often indications of mature genius and energy. We should encourage an early taste for reading but not censure their choice of literature. Above all, we should excite their desire for knowledge by showing its intrinsic excellence.

Godwin however goes on to suggest that if a pupil learns only because he or she desires it the whole formidable apparatus of education might be swept away. No figures such as teacher or pupil would then be left; each would be glad in cases of difficulty to consult a person more informed than him or herself but there would no longer be any leaders or led. In a free society, no one would be expected to learn anything unless they desired it while everyone would be prepared to offer guidance and encouragement when requested. In this way, the mind would develop according to its natural tendencies and children would be able to develop fully their potential.

While Godwin does not offer a blueprint of his free society—to do so would be opposed to his whole scheme of progress and his notion of truth—he does outline some of the general directions it might take. In the first place, he is careful to show that freedom does not mean licence, that is to say, to act as one pleases without being accountable to the principles of reason. He distinguishes between two sorts of independence: natural independence, 'a freedom from all constraint, except that of reasons and inducements presented to the understanding', which is of the utmost importance; and moral independence, which is always injurious. It is essential that we should be free to cultivate our individuality, and to follow the dictates of our own understanding, but we should be ready to judge and influence the actions of each other. External freedom is of little value without moral growth; indeed, it is possible for a person to be physically enslaved and yet retain his sense of independence while an unconstrained person can voluntarily enslave himself through passive obedience. For Godwin civil liberty is thus not an end in itself, but a means to personal growth in wisdom and virtue.

Godwin did not call himself an anarchist and used the word 'anarchy' like his contemporaries in a negative sense to denote the violent and extreme disorder which might follow the immediate dissolution of government without a general acceptance of the principles of political justice. In such a situation, he feared that some enraged elements might threaten personal security and free enquiry. The example of the French revolutionaries had shown him that 'ungoverned passions will often not stop at equality, but incite them to grasp at power'. And yet Godwin saw the mischiefs of 'anarchy' in this sense as preferable to those of despotism. A state of despotism is permanent, while anarchy is transitory. Anarchy moreover diffuses energy and enterprise through the community and disengages men from prejudice and implicit faith. Above all, it has a 'distorted and tremendous likeness of truth and liberty' and can lead to the best form of human society. It was always Godwin's contention that society for the greater part carries on its own peaceful and productive organization.

In place of modern nation states with their complex apparatus of government, Godwin proposes a decentralized and simplified society of face-to-face communities. The ideas of 'great empire and legislative unity' are for Godwin plainly the 'barbarous remains of the days of military heroism'. It is preferable to decentralize power since neighbours are best informed of each other's concerns and since sobriety and equity are the obvious characteristics of a limited circle. People should therefore form a voluntary federation of districts (a 'confederacy of lesser republics') in order to coordinate production and secure social benefits. In such a pluralistic commonwealth, Godwin suggests that the basic social unit might be a small territory like the traditional English 'parish'—the self-managing commune of later anarchists. Democracy would be direct and participatory so that the voice of reason could be heard and spoken by all citizens. Such a decentralized society need not however be 'parochial' in the pejorative sense since with the ending of nation states and their rivalries the whole human species would constitute 'one great republic'.

Godwin recognizes that in a transitional period, a modified form of government might be necessary in order to solve disputes between districts or to repel a foreign invader. He therefore suggests that districts might send delegates to a general assembly or congress of the federation but such a measure should be employed as sparingly as possible and only in exceptional emergencies. The congress moreover would form no permanent or common centre of authority and any officials would be supported voluntarily.

At the local level, popular juries could be set up to deal with controversies and injustices among individuals within the community. Cases would be judged according to their particular circumstances in the light of the general good. But in the long run, both assemblies and juries would lose any authority and it would suffice to invite districts to co-operate for the common advantage or offenders to forsake their errors. The coercion of law would be replaced by the persuasion of public opinion. Simplify the social system, and Godwin was confident that the voice of reason could be heard, consensus achieved and the natural harmony of interests prevail. As people became accustomed to governing themselves, all coercive bodies would become superfluous, and government would give way to the spontaneously ordered society of anarchy. People would live simple but cultivated lives in open families in harmony with nature. Marriage would disappear and be replaced by free unions; their offspring would be cared for and educated by the community.

In such a free and equal society, there would be the opportunity for everyone to develop their sympathies and minds. With the abolition of the complicated machinery of government, the end to excessive luxuries and the sharing of work by all, the labour required to produce the necessaries of life would be drastically reduced—possibly, Godwin calculates, to half an hour a day. Far from ignoring the Industrial Revolution, Godwin further looks to technology—'various sorts of mills, weaving engines, steam engines' and even one day an automatic plough—to reduce and alleviate unpleasant toil. Unlike Tolstoy he saw no dignity in unnecessary manual labour. This system of production would not only lessen the enforced co-operation imposed by the present division of labour, but increase the immeasurable wealth of leisure to cultivate our minds. Science moreover might one day make mind omnipotent over matter, prolong life, and, Godwin suggests in a rare flight of wild conjecture, even discover the secret of immortality!

Although Godwin's decentralized society finds undoubtedly some inspiration in the organic communities of pre-industrial England, it is by no means a purely agrarian vision.[10] His confidence in the potential liberating effects of modern technology and science shows that he was not looking backwards but forward to the future. Indeed, while the nineteenth and early twentieth centuries saw increased centralization

---

10 Cf. Kramnick, Introduction to *P.J.*, 52; Don Locke, *A Fantasy of Reason: The Life and Thought of William Godwin* (London: Routledge Kegan and Paul, 1980), 348.

of production, the new technology may well as Godwin hoped lead to a dissolution of monolithic industries and a break-up of great cities.[11] His vision of small-scale production for the local market comes close to Kropotkin's *Fields, Factories and Workshops Tomorrow*.[12]

While he does not enter into details, Godwin implies that production would be organized voluntarily, with workers pursuing their interests or talents. A certain division of labour might still exist, since people with particular skills and interests might prefer to spend their time in specialized work. The producer would control distribution and there would be a voluntary sharing of material goods. Workers would give their surplus to those who needed them and would receive what was necessary to satisfy their own needs from the surplus of their neighbours. In this way goods would pass spontaneously to where they were most needed and a central storehouse would be unnecessary. Economic relationships however would always be based on free distribution and not barter or exchange.

Godwin was anxious to define carefully the subtle connection between the individual and group in such a free and equal society. His position has been seriously misunderstood for he has been accused of wanting to submerge the individual in communal solidarity.[13]

It is true that Godwin wrote 'everything that is usually understood by the term co-operation is, in some degree, an evil'. But the co-operation he condemns is the uniform activity enforced by the division of labour, by a restrictive association or by those in power. He could not understand why we must always be obliged to consult the convenience of others or be reduced to a 'clockwork uniformity'. For this reason, he saw no need for common labour, meals or stores in an equal society; they are 'mistaken instruments for restraining the conduct without making conquest of the judgement'.

It is also true that society for Godwin forms no organic whole and is nothing much more than the sum of its individuals. He pictured the enlightened person making individual calculations of pleasure and pain and carefully weighing up the consequences of his or her actions. He

---

11 Cf. Woodcock, *Anarchism*, 83n.
12 Peter Kropotkin, *Fields, Factories and Workshops Tomorrow*, ed. Colin Ward (London: Freedom Press, 1985); originally published in 1898.
13 Kramnick, Introduction to *P.J.*, 52.

stressed the value of autonomy for intellectual and moral development; we all require a sphere of discretion, a mental space for creative thought. He could see no value in losing oneself in the existence of another: 'Every man', he wrote, 'ought to rest upon his own centre, and consult his own understanding. Every man ought to feel his independence, that he can assert the principles of justice and truth without being obliged treacherously to adapt them to the peculiarities of his situation and the errors of others.'

This recognition of the need for individual autonomy should be borne in mind when considering one of the major criticisms levelled at Godwin; that the tyranny of public opinion could be more dangerous than that of law in his anarchist society.[14] Godwin certainly argues that we all have a duty to amend the errors and promote the welfare of our neighbours; that we must practise perfect sincerity at all times.

Indeed, he goes so far as to suggest that the 'general inspection' which would replace public authority would provide a force 'no less irresistible than whips and chains' to reform conduct.

Now while this might sound distinctly illiberal, Godwin made clear that he was totally opposed to any collective vigilance which might tyrannize the individual or impose certain ideas and values. In the first place, the kind of sincerity he recommends is not intended to turn neighbours into priggish busybodies but to release them from their unnecessary repressions so that they might be 'truly friends with each other'.[15] Secondly, any censure we might offer to our neighbours would be an appeal to their reason and be offered in a mild and affectionate way. Thirdly, Godwin assumes that people will be rational and independent individuals who recognize each other's autonomy: 'My neighbour may censure me freely and without reserve, but he should remember that I am to act by my deliberation and not his.'[16]

While Godwin certainly values individual autonomy it is somewhat unfair however to argue that Godwin's 'great failing' is his 'lack of understanding of the social nature of humanity'.[17] He repeatedly stresses

---

14 Woodcock, *Anarchism*, 78–79.
15 *P.J.*, (1798) I, 335.
16 *P.J.*, (1798) I, 168.
17 John P. Clark, *The Philosophical Anarchism of William Godwin* (Princeton, NJ: Princeton University Press, 1977), 311–12.

that we are social beings, that we are made for society, and that society brings out our best qualities. Indeed, he sees no tension or contradiction between autonomy and collectivity since 'the love of liberty obviously leads to a sentiment of union, and a disposition to sympathize in the concerns of others'. Godwin's novels show only too vividly the psychological and moral dangers of excessive solitude and isolation. His whole ethical system of universal benevolence is moreover inspired by a love for others.

In fact, in a free and equal society Godwin believes people would be both more social and individual: 'each man would be united to his neighbour, in love and mutual kindness, a thousand times more than now: but each man would think and judge for himself'. Ultimately, the individual and group are not opposed for the individual would become more truly himself as well as more socially conscious; the 'narrow principle of selfishness' would vanish and 'each would lose his individual existence, in the thought of the general good'. It is precisely Godwin's greatest strength that he manages in this way to reconcile the claims of individual autonomy and the demands of social life. As such, Godwin's anarchism is closer to the communism of Kropotkin than the egoism of Stirner or the competition of Proudhon.

Perhaps though his greatest failing is his lack of ecological awareness. He wrote that 'the earth is the sufficient means, either by the fruit it produces, or the animals it breeds, of the subsistence of man'. He was largely right about population—it can be controlled by artificial means and moral restraint and it tends to go down in societies which are more equal. But he was wrong at the beginning of the Industrial Revolution about the injurious impact of human beings on the well-being of the land, sea and air. Advocates of social or liberation ecology and of animal liberation would hardly agree with his expressed sentiment. We now know that there are severe limits to how much the earth can produce and how much human population it can support. As a humanist, his consciousness and sensibility ultimately failed him when it came to the welfare of other species and to our place deep within nature.

Again, while Godwin offers a subtle and compelling vision of a free and equal society, he offers little advice about the way we are to achieve it. He did not rest his hopes like Bakunin on a cataclysmic upheaval but on the gradual reformation of the human personality which has been weighed down for centuries by authoritarian institutions and blind

prejudice. But while his gradualism shows that he was no naive visionary, it does give a conservative turn to his practical politics. He believed
that it was necessary to postpone revolution and condemned all isolated
attempts at protest and change. Instead, he felt it was right to support
any political movement which seemed to be expanding human freedom
and in his own day supported the Whigs in Parliament. But having
shown so eloquently the disastrous effects of political authority and
economic inequality, his position forced him apparently to abandon
generations to a life of suffering until things improved.

Godwin's reliance on informal enlightenment and education as
the means of reform also throws up an inconsistency in his analysis of
history and society. He stressed how ideas and values are shaped by circumstances, particularly by economic and political factors. But having
demonstrated the interaction between consciousness and circumstances,
Godwin chose to tackle reform primarily in the realm of consciousness
instead of on both fronts. He was left with the dilemma that human
beings cannot become wholly rational as long as government exists, yet
government must exist while human beings remain irrational. Both in
his theory and his life, he failed to develop an adequate praxis.

Since Godwin anarchist theory has developed other strategies for
social change, ranging from the general strike through civil disobedience to direct action. Most anarchists recognize the need to change
consciousness as well as to create new forms of living. There are good
grounds for trying to open up where possible free zones within capitalist or authoritarian states in order to demonstrate how a free society
might develop. There is also room for a whole variety of social experiments and economic initiatives based on the principles of self-manage-
ment and direct democracy. Nevertheless, while anarchist forms have
become richer and their tactics more varied, Godwin gave in his small,
independent circle of devoted guides the model of the classic anarchist
group which consists of a loose and voluntary association of free and
equal individuals. His stress on political education finds echoes in the
anarchist doctrine of 'propaganda by the word'. Above all, by stressing
that moral regeneration must precede economic and political reform he
speaks directly to those who believe that the 'political is the personal'.

From the foregoing analysis, it should be clear that Godwin is not
only a social and political philosopher on a par with Hobbes, Locke,
Rousseau and Mill, but the most consistent and profound exponent

of philosophical anarchism. With closely reasoned arguments he carefully draws his anarchist conclusions from a clear and plausible view of human nature and society. He believes that politics is inseparable from ethics, and offers a persuasive view of justice. His criticisms of fundamental assumptions in law, government and democracy are full of insight. From a sound view of truth, he develops one of the most trenchant defences of the freedom of thought and expression ever written.

In place of existing tyrannies, he proposes a decentralized and simplified society which is both free and equal as the most desirable form of human existence. In his educational theory, he shows the evils of authoritarian teaching and the benefits of learning through desire. In his economics, he demonstrates the disastrous effects of economic inequality and outlines a system of voluntary communism. And if his practical politics are inadequate, it is because he is primarily a philosopher concerned with the validity of universal principles rather than with their specific application.

In short, Godwin will be of interest to all those who believe that freedom, individuality, social justice, rationality, happiness and sincerity are central concerns of human enquiry and endeavour. He will appeal to those who recognize that truth and enlightenment can only emerge through the free clash of ideas and values and that overall harmony can best be achieved through social pluralism and cultural diversity. He will inspire all those free spirits who uphold that government is an unnecessary evil and that human beings flourish best when least interfered with by coercive institutions. By the intrepid deduction from first principles, Godwin went beyond the radicalism of his age to become the first great anarchist thinker. He still remains today the most profound and compelling.

SELECTIONS

I

SUMMARY OF PRINCIPLES[1]

ESTABLISHED AND REASONED UPON IN THE FOLLOWING WORK.

The reader who would form a just estimate of the reasonings of these volumes, cannot perhaps proceed more judiciously, than by examining for himself the truth of these principles, and the support they afford to the various inferences interspersed through the work.

The true object of moral and political disquisition, is pleasure or happiness.

The primary, or earliest class of human pleasures, is the pleasures of the external senses.

In addition to these, man is susceptible of certain secondary pleasures, as the pleasures of intellectual feeling, the pleasures of sympathy, and the pleasures of self-approbation.

The secondary pleasures are probably more exquisite than the primary:

Or, at least,

The most desirable state of man, is that, in which he has access to all these sources of pleasure, and is in possession of a happiness the most varied and uninterrupted.

This state is a state of high civilisation.

II
The most desirable condition of the human species, is a state of society.

The injustice and violence of men in a state of society, produced the demand for government.

---

1   *P.J,* (1798), xxiii–xxvii.

Government, as it was forced upon mankind by their vices, so has it commonly been the creature of their ignorance and mistake.

Government was intended to suppress injustice, but it offers new occasions and temptations for the commission of it.

By concentrating the force of the community, it gives occasion to wild projects of calamity, to oppression, despotism, war, and conquest.

By perpetuating and aggravating the inequality of property, it fosters many injurious passions, and excites men to the practice of robbery and fraud.

Government was intended to suppress injustice, but its effect has been to embody and perpetuate it.

III

The immediate object of government, is security.

The means employed by government, is restriction, an abridgment of individual independence.

The pleasures of self-approbation, together with the right cultivation of all our pleasures require individual independence.

Without independence men cannot become either wise, or useful, or happy.

Consequently, the most desirable state of mankind, is that which maintains general security, with the smallest incroachment upon individual independence.

IV

The true standard of the conduct of one man towards another, is justice.

Justice is a principle which proposes to itself the production of the greatest sum of pleasure or happiness.

Justice requires that I should put myself in the place of an impartial spectator of human concerns, and divest myself of retrospect to my own predilections.

Justice is a rule of the utmost universality, and prescribes a specific mode of proceeding, in all affairs by which the happiness of a human being may be affected.

V

Duty is that mode of action, which constitutes the best application of the capacity of the individual, to the general advantage.

Right is the claim of the individual, to his share of the benefit arising from his neighbours' discharge of their several duties.

The claim of the individual, is either to the exertion or the forbearance of his neighbours.

The exertions of men in society should ordinarily be trusted to their discretion; their forbearance, in certain cases, is a point of more pressing necessity, and is the direct province of political superintendence, or government.

VI

The voluntary actions of men are under the direction of their feelings.

Reason is not an independent principle, and has no tendency to excite us to action; in a practical view, it is merely a comparison and balancing of different feelings.

Reason, though it cannot excite us to action, is calculated to regulate our conduct according to the comparative worth it ascribes to different excitements.

It is to the improvement of reason therefore, that we are to look for the improvement of our social condition.

VII

Reason depends for its clearness and strength upon the cultivation of knowledge.

The extent of our progress in the cultivation of knowledge is unlimited.

Hence it follows,

1. That human inventions, and the modes of social existence, are susceptible of perpetual improvement.
2. That institutions calculated to give perpetuity to any particular mode of thinking, or condition of existence, are pernicious.

VIII

The pleasures of intellectual feeling, and the pleasures of self-approbation, together with the right cultivation of all our pleasures, are connected with soundness of understanding.

Soundness of understanding is inconsistent with prejudice: consequently, as few falsehoods as possible, either speculative or practical, should be fostered among mankind.

Soundness of understanding is connected with freedom of enquiry: consequently, opinion should, as far as public security will admit, be exempted from restraint.

Soundness of understanding is connected with simplicity of manners, and leisure for intellectual cultivation: consequently, a distribution of property extremely unequal, is adverse to the most desirable state of man.

II

HUMAN NATURE

1 Necessity and Free Will

Freedom of the will is absurdly represented as necessary to render the mind susceptible of moral principles; but in reality, so far as we act with liberty, so far as we are independent of motives, our conduct is as independent of morality as it is of reason, nor is it possible that we should deserve either praise or blame for a proceeding thus capricious and indisciplinable.[1]

Free will is an integral part of the science of man, and may be said to constitute its most important chapter. . . . [It] lies at the foundation of our moral energies, fills us with a moral enthusiasm, prompts all our animated exertions on the theatre of the world, whether upon a wide or a narrow scale, and penetrates us with the most lively and fervent approbation or disapprobation of the acts of ourselves and others in which the forwarding or obstructing [of] human happiness is involved.

But, though the language of the necessarian [or determinist] is at war with the indestructible feelings of the human mind, and though his demonstrations will for ever crumble into dust, when brought to the test of the activity of real life, yet his doctrines, to the reflecting and enlightened, will by no means be without their use. In the sobriety of the closet, we inevitably assent to his conclusions; nor is it easy to conceive how a rational man and a philosopher abstractedly can entertain a doubt of the necessity of human actions.[2]

---

1   *P.J.*, (1798) Bk. IV, ch. vii; hereafter the edition referred to is the 1798 one unless otherwise stated. The punctuation has been slightly changed to improve the flow and in a few cases the spelling has been modernized.

2   *T.M.*, 239.

2 The Characters of Men Originate in their External Circumstances

This view of things presents us with an idea of the universe, as of a body of events in systematical arrangement, nothing in the boundless progress of things interrupting this system, or breaking in upon the experienced succession of antecedents and consequents. In the life of every human being there is a chain of events, generated in the lapse of ages which preceded his birth, and going on in regular procession through the whole period of his existence, in consequence of which it was impossible for him to act in any instance otherwise than he has acted.[3]

The actions and dispositions of men are not the offspring of any original bias that they bring into the world in favour of one sentiment or character rather than another, but flow entirely from the operation of circumstances and events acting upon a faculty of receiving sensible impressions.[4]

Consider, that man is but a machine! He is just what his nature and circumstances have made him: he obeys the necessities which he cannot resist. If he is corrupt, it is because he has been corrupted. If he is unamiable, it is because he has been 'mocked, and spitefully entreated, and spit upon'. Give him a different education, place him under other circumstances, treat him with as much gentleness and generosity, as he has experienced of harshness, and he would be altogether a different creature.[5]

We shall . . . unquestionably, as our minds grow enlarged, be brought to the entire and unreserved conviction that man is a machine, that he is governed by external impulses, and is to be regarded as the medium only through the intervention of which previously existing causes are enabled to produce certain effects. We shall see, according to an expressive phrase, that he 'could not help it', and, of consequence, while we look down from the high tower of philosophy upon the scene of human affairs, our prevailing emotion will be pity, even towards the criminal,

---

3   *P.J.*, Bk. IV, ch. viii.
4   *P.J.*, Bk. I, ch. iv.
5   William Godwin, *Mandeville: A Tale of the Seventeenth Century*, Vol. II (Edinburgh: Archibald Constable and Co., 1817), 143.

who, from the qualities he brought into the world, and the various circumstances which act upon him from infancy, and form his character, is impelled to be the means of the evils, which we view with so profound disapprobation, and the existence of which we so entirely regret.[6]

3 The Voluntary Actions of Men Originate in their Opinions

The distinction between voluntary and involuntary action, if properly stated, is exceedingly simple. That action is involuntary which takes place in us either without foresight on our part, or contrary to the full bent of our inclinations. Thus, if a child or a person of mature age burst into tears in a manner unexpected or unforeseen by himself, or if he burst into tears though his pride or any other principle make him exert every effort to restrain them, this action is involuntary. Voluntary action is where the event is foreseen previously to its occurrence, and the hope or fear of that event forms the excitement, or, as it is most frequently termed, the motive, inducing us, if hope be the passion, to endeavour to forward, and, if fear, to endeavour to prevent it. It is this motion, in this manner generated, to which we annex the idea of voluntariness.[7]

In the meantime it is obvious to remark that the perfection of the human character consists in approaching as nearly as possible to the perfectly voluntary state. We ought to be upon all occasions prepared to render a reason of our actions. We should remove ourselves to the furthest distance from the state of mere inanimate machines, acted upon by causes of which they have no understanding. We should be cautious of thinking it a sufficient reason for an action that we are accustomed to perform it, and that we once thought it right. The human understanding has so powerful a tendency to improvement that it is more than probable that, in many instances, the arguments which once appeared to us sufficient would upon re-examination appear inadequate and futile. We should therefore subject them to perpetual revisal. In our speculative opinions and our practical principles we should never consider the book of enquiry as shut. We should accustom ourselves not to forget the reasons that produced our determination, but be ready upon all occasions clearly to announce and fully to enumerate them. . . . All the

---

6   *T.M.*, 240.
7   *P.J.*, Bk. I, ch. v.

most important occasions of our lives are capable of being subjected at pleasure to a decision, as nearly as possible, perfectly voluntary. Still it remains true that, when the understanding clearly perceives rectitude, propriety and eligibility to belong to a certain conduct, and so long as it has that perception, that conduct will infallibly be adopted. A perception of truth will inevitably be produced by a clear evidence brought home to the understanding, and the constancy of the perception will be proportioned to the apprehended value of the thing perceived. Reason therefore and conviction still appear to be the proper instrument, and the sufficient instrument for regulating the actions of mankind.[8]

4 Equality

Notwithstanding the encroachments that have been made upon the equality of mankind, a great and substantial equality remains. There is no such disparity among the human race as to enable one man to hold several other men in subjection, except so far as they are willing to be subject. The moral equality is still less open to reasonable exception. . . . By moral equality I understand the propriety of applying one unalterable rule of justice to every case that may arise. This cannot be questioned, but upon arguments that would subvert the very nature of virtue. . . . Justice has relation to beings endowed with perception, and capable of pleasure and pain. Now it immediately results from the nature of such beings, independently of arbitrary constitution, that pleasure is agreeable and pain odious, pleasure to be desired and pain to be disapproved. It is therefore just and reasonable that such beings should contribute, so far as it lies in their power, to the pleasure and benefit of each other. . . .[9]

From these simple principles we may deduce the moral equality of mankind. We are partakers of a common nature, and the same causes that contribute to the benefit of one will contribute to the benefit of another. Our senses and faculties are of the same denomination. Our pleasures and pains will therefore be alike. We are all of us endowed with reason, able to compare, to judge and to infer. The improvement therefore which is to be desired for one is to be desired for another.

8   *P.J.*, Bk. I, ch. v.
9   *P.J.*, Bk. II, ch. iii.

The system of political imposture divides men into two classes, one of which is to think and reason for the whole, and the other to take the conclusions of their superiors on trust. This distinction is not founded in the nature of things; there is no such inherent difference between man and man as it thinks proper to suppose. Nor is it less injurious than it is unfounded. The two classes which it creates must be more and less than man. It is too much to expect of the former, while we consign to them an unnatural monopoly, that they should rigidly consult for the good of the whole. It is an iniquitous requisition upon the latter that they should never employ their understandings, or penetrate into the essences of things, but always rest in a deceitful appearance.[10]

There is no state of mankind that renders them incapable of the exercise of reason. There is no period in which it is necessary to hold the human species in a condition of pupillage. If there were, it would seem but reasonable that their superintendents and guardians, as in the case of infants of another sort, should provide for the means of their subsistence without calling upon them for the exertions of their own understanding. Wherever men are competent to look the first duties of humanity in the face, and to provide for their defence against the invasions of hunger and the inclemencies of the sky, it can scarcely be thought that they are not equally capable of every other exertion that may be essential to their security and welfare.[11]

All men are acknowledged to partake of a common nature, to have a right to deliberate respecting of their system of action; and, having deliberated, to conduct themselves accordingly. This is the most important revolution that has occurred in the history of the world. The equality of human beings as such, opens up on us the prospect of perpetual improvement. It is of consequence not true that the mass of our species is to be held for ever in leading-strings, while a few only are to have the prerogative of thinking and directing for all, but that the whole community is to run the generous race for intellectual and moral superiority. This thought lies at the foundation of all improvement. It opens to

---

10 *P.J.*, Bk. V, ch. xv.
11 *P.J.*, Bk. I, ch. vi.

us the prospect of indefinite advancement in sound judgement, in real science, and the just conduct of our social institutions.[12]

5 Individuality and Society

It is a curious subject to enquire into the due medium between individuality and concert. On the one hand, it is to be observed that human beings are formed for society. Without society, we shall probably be deprived of the most eminent enjoyments of which our nature is susceptible. In society, no man possessing the genuine marks of a man can stand alone. Our opinions, our tempers and our habits are modified by those of each other. This is by no means the mere operation of arguments and persuasives; it occurs in that insensible and gradual way which no resolution can enable us wholly to counteract. He that would attempt to counteract it by insulating himself will fall into a worse error than that which he seeks to avoid. He will divest himself of the character of a man, and be incapable of judging his fellow men, or of reasoning upon human affairs.

On the other hand, individuality is of the very essence of intellectual excellence. He that resigns himself wholly to sympathy and imitation can possess little of mental strength or accuracy. The system of his life is a species of sensual dereliction. . . . The truly venerable, and the truly happy, must have the fortitude to maintain his individuality. If he indulge in the gratifications, and cultivate the feelings of man, he must at the same time be strenuous in following the train of his disquisitions, and exercising the powers of his understanding.[13]

Society is the source of innumerable pleasures; without society we can scarcely be said to live; yet in how many ways does society infringe upon the independence and peace of its members. Man delights to control and to inforce submission upon his fellow-man; human creatures desire to exercise lordship and to display authority. One class and division of the community, is taught to think its interests adverse to the interest of another class and division of the community. The institution of property has been the source of much improvement and much admirable

---

12 *P.J.*, Bk. VIII, ch. viii Appendix.
13 William Godwin, *Of Population* (London: Longman, Hurst, Bees, Orme and Brown, 1820), 614.

activity to mankind; yet how many evils to multitudes of our species have sprung from the institution of property. The same may be said of the inequality of conditions.[14]

No doubt man is formed for society. But there is a way in which for a man to lose his own existence in that of others, that is eminently vicious and detrimental. Every man ought to rest upon his own centre, and consult his own understanding. Every man ought to feel his independence, that he can assert the principles of justice and truth, without being obliged treacherously to adapt them to the peculiarities of his situation, and the errors of others.[15]

Man is especially characterised by two propensities—the love of society, and the love of solitude. The former is perhaps the most essential to us, since the great bulk of ordinary men live almost perpetually in society; and I do not know that they are apt to be unhappy for want of ever being alone. Society is our proper sphere. All our great lessons from youth to age are learned in society; in society all our sweetest affections are called into play, and our main virtues are exercised. But the man of refinement, at least, can scarcely live without occasional intervals of solitude.[16]

6 Perfectibility

The corollaries respecting political truth, deducible from the simple proposition . . . that the voluntary actions of men, are in all instances conformable to the deductions of their understanding, are of the highest importance. Hence we may infer what are the hopes and prospects of human improvement. The doctrine which may be founded upon these principles may perhaps best be expressed in the five following propositions: Sound reasoning and truth, when adequately communicated, must always be victorious over error: Sound reasoning and truth are capable of being so communicated: Truth is omnipotent: The vices and moral weakness of man are not invincible: Man is perfectible, or in other words susceptible of perpetual improvement.[17]

---

14 *P.J.*, Bk. VIII, ch. vi.
15 *Essays*, 219.
16 *Essays*, 6.
17 *P.J.*, Bk. I, ch. v.

By perfectible, it is not meant that he is capable of being brought to perfection. But the word seems sufficiently adapted to express the faculty of being continually made better and receiving perpetual improvement; and in this sense it is here to be understood. The term perfectible, thus explained, not only does not imply the capacity of being brought to perfection, but stands in express opposition to it. If we could arrive at perfection, there would be an end to our improvement. There is however one thing of great importance that it does imply: every perfection or excellence that human beings are competent to conceive, human beings, unless in cases that are palpably and unequivocally excluded by the structure of their frame, are competent to attain.[18]

There is, in reality, little room for scepticism respecting the omnipotence of truth. Truth is the pebble in the lake; and, however slowly, in the present case, the circles succeed each other, they will infallibly go on, till they overspread the surface. No order of mankind will for ever remain ignorant of the principles of justice, equality and public good. No sooner will they understand them than they will perceive the coincidence of virtue and public good with private interest: nor will any erroneous establishment be able effectually to support itself against general opinion. In this contest sophistry will vanish, and mischievous institutions sink quietly into neglect. Truth will bring down all her forces, mankind will be her army, and oppression, injustice, monarchy and vice, will tumble into a common ruin.[19]

Man is to a considerable degree the artificer of his own fortune. We can apply our reflections and our ingenuity to the remedy of whatever we regret. Speaking in a general way, and within certain liberal and expansive limitations, it should appear that there is no evil under which the human species can labour, that man is not competent to cure.[20]

Man is a rational being. It is by this particular that he is eminently distinguished from the brute creation. He collects premises and deduces conclusions. He enters into systems of thinking, and combines systems

---

18　*P.J.*, Bk. I, ch. v.
19　*P.J.*, Bk. V, ch. viii.
20　*Of Population*, 615.

of action, which he pursues from day to day, and from year to year. It is by this feature in his constitution that he becomes emphatically the subject of history, of poetry and fiction. It is by this that he is raised above the other inhabitants of the globe of earth, and that the individuals of our race are made the partners of 'gods, and men like gods'.[21]

Let then no man, in the supercilious spirit of a fancied disdain, allow himself to detract from our common nature. We are ourselves the models of all the excellence that the human mind can conceive. There have been men, whose virtues may well redeem all the contempt with which satire and detraction have sought to overwhelm our species. There have been memorable periods in the history of man, when the best, the most generous and exalted sentiments have swallowed up and obliterated all that was of an opposite character. And it is but just, that those by whom these things are fairly considered, should anticipate the progress of our nature, and believe that human understanding and human virtue will hereafter accomplish such things as the heart of man has never yet been daring enough to conceive.[22]

---

21 *T.M.*, 93.
22 *T.M.*, 470–71.

III

ETHICS

1 Morality

[Politics] is strictly speaking a department of the science of morals. Morality is the source from which its fundamental axioms must be drawn, and they will be made somewhat clearer in the present instance if we assume the term justice as a general appellation for all moral duty.[1]

Morality is that system of conduct which is determined by a consideration of the greatest general good: he is entitled to the highest moral approbation whose conduct is, in the greatest number of instances, or in the most momentous instances, governed by views of benevolence, and made subservient to public utility.[2]

Morality is nothing else but that system which teaches us to contribute upon all occasions, to the extent of our power, to the well-being and happiness of every intellectual and sensitive existence. But there is no action of our lives which does not in some way affect that happiness. Our property, our time, and our faculties may all of them be made to contribute to this end.[3]

The end of virtue is to add to the sum of pleasurable sensation. The beacon and regulator of virtue is impartiality, that we shall not give that exertion to procure the pleasure of an individual which might have been employed in procuring the pleasure of many individuals.[4]

---

1   *P.J.*, Bk. II, ch. ii.
2   *P.J.*, Bk. II, ch. i.
3   *P.J.*, Bk. II, ch. v.
4   *P.J.*, Bk. VIII, ch. vii.

Pleasure and pain, happiness and misery, constitute the whole ultimate subject of moral enquiry. There is nothing desirable but the obtaining of the one and the avoiding of the other. All the researches of human imagination cannot add a single article to this summary of good.[5]

The nature of happiness and misery, pleasure and pain, is independent of positive institution. It is immutably true that whatever tends to procure a balance of the former is to be desired, and whatever tends to procure a balance of the latter is to be rejected.[6]

Good is a general name, including pleasure, and the means by which pleasure is procured. Evil is a general name, including pain, and the means by which pain is produced. Of the two things included in these general names, the first is cardinal and substantive, the second has no intrinsic recommendations, but depends for its value on the other. Pleasure therefore is to be termed an absolute good; the means of pleasure are only relatively good. The same observation may be stated of pain.[7]

This criterion [of virtue] has been above described, and it is not perhaps of the utmost importance whether we call it utility, or justice, or, more periphrastically, the production of the greatest general good, the greatest public sum of pleasurable sensation. Call it by what name you please, it will still be true that this is the law by which our actions must be tried.[8]

2 Moral Rules

Let us enquire then into the nature and origin of general principles. Engaged, as men are, in perpetual intercourse with their neighbours, and constantly liable to be called upon without the smallest previous notice, in cases where the interest of their fellows is deeply involved, it is not possible for them, upon all occasions, to deduce, through a chain of reasoning, the judgment which should be followed. Hence the necessity of resting-places for the mind, of deductions, already stored in the

---

5   *P.J.*, Bk. III, ch. iii.
6   *P.J.*, Bk. II, ch. vi.
7   *P.J.*, Bk. IV, ch. xi.
8   *Thoughts* (1801), 34.

memory, and prepared for application as circumstances may demand. We find this necessity equally urgent upon us in matters of science and abstraction as in conduct and morals. Theory has also a further use. It serves as a perpetual exercise and aliment to the understanding, and renders us competent and vigorous to judge in every situation that can occur. Nothing can be more idle and shallow than the competition which some men have set up between theory and practice. It is true that we can never predict, from theory alone, the success of any given experiment. It is true that no theory, accurately speaking, can possibly be practical. It is the business of theory to collect the circumstances of a certain set of cases, and arrange them. It would cease to be theory if it did not leave out many circumstances; it collects such as are general, and leaves out such as are particular. In practice, however, those circumstances inevitably arise which are necessarily omitted in the general process: they cause the phenomenon, in various ways, to include features which were not in the prediction, and to be diversified in those that were. Yet theory is of the highest use; and those who decry it may even be proved not to understand themselves. They do not mean that men should always act in a particular case, without illustration from any other case, for that would be to deprive us of all understanding. The moment we begin to compare cases, and infer, we begin to theorize; no two things in the universe were ever perfectly alike. The genuine exercise of man therefore is to theorize, for this is, in other words, to sharpen and improve his intellect; but not to become the slave of theory, or at any time to forget that it is, by its very nature, precluded from comprehending the whole of what claims our attention.

To apply this to the case of morals. General principles of morality are so far valuable as they truly delineate the means of utility, pleasure or happiness. But every action of any human being has its appropriate result; and, the more closely it is examined, the more truly will that result appear. General rules and theories are not infallible. It would be preposterous to suppose that, in order to judge fairly, and conduct myself properly, I ought only to look at a thing from a certain distance, and not consider it minutely. On the contrary, I ought, as far as lies in my power, to examine everything upon its own grounds, and decide concerning it upon its own merits. To rest in general rules is sometimes a necessity which our imperfection imposes upon us, and sometimes the refuge of our indolence; but the true dignity of human reason is, as much as we are able, to go beyond them, to have our faculties in act upon every occasion that occurs, and to conduct ourselves accordingly. . . .

The remote consequences of an action, especially as they relate to the fulfilling, or not fulfilling, the expectation excited . . . depend chiefly on general circumstances, and not upon particulars; belong to the class, and not to the individual. But this makes no essential alteration in what was before delivered. It will still be incumbent on us, when called into action, to estimate the nature of the particular case, that we may ascertain where the urgency of special circumstances is such as to supersede rules that are generally obligatory.[9]

3 Justice

By justice I understand that impartial treatment of every man in matters that relate to his happiness, which is measured solely by a consideration of the properties of the receiver, and the capacity of him that bestows. Its principle therefore is, according to a well known phrase, to be 'no respecter of persons'.

Considerable light will probably be thrown upon our investigation if, quitting for the present the political view, we examine justice merely as it exists among individuals. Justice is a rule of conduct originating in the connection of one percipient being with another. A comprehensive maxim which has been laid down upon the subject is 'that we should love our neighbour as ourselves'. But this maxim, though possessing considerable merit as a popular principle, is not modelled with the strictness of philosophical accuracy.

In a loose and general view I and my neighbour are both of us men; and of consequence entitled to equal attention. But, in reality, it is probable that one of us is a being of more worth and importance than the other. A man is of more worth than a beast; because, being possessed of higher faculties, he is capable of a more refined and genuine happiness. In the same manner the illustrious archbishop of Cambray [Fénelon] was of more worth than his valet, and there are few of us that would hesitate to pronounce, if his palace were in flames, and the life of only one of them could be preserved, which of the two ought to be preferred.

But there is another ground of preference, beside the private consideration of one of them being further removed from the state of a

9 *P.J.*, Bk. IV, ch. vi Appendix 1.

mere animal. We are not connected with one or two percipient beings, but with a society, a nation, and in some sense with the whole family of mankind. Of consequence that life ought to be preferred which will be most conducive to the general good. In saving the life of Fénelon, suppose at the moment he conceived the project of his immortal Telemachus, I should have been promoting the benefit of thousands who have been cured by the perusal of that work of some error, vice and consequent unhappiness. Nay, my benefit would extend further than this; for every individual, thus cured, has become a better member of society, and has contributed in his turn to the happiness, information and improvement of others.

Suppose I had been myself the valet; I ought to have chosen to die, rather than Fénelon should have died. The life of Fénelon was really preferable to that of the valet. But understanding is the faculty that perceives the truth of this and similar propositions; and justice is the principle that regulates my conduct accordingly. It would have been just in the valet to have preferred the archbishop to himself. To have done otherwise would have been a breach of justice.

Suppose the valet had been my brother, my father or my benefactor. This would not alter the truth of the proposition. The life of Fénelon would still be more valuable than that of the valet; and justice, pure, unadulterated justice, would still have preferred that which was the most valuable. Justice would have taught me to save the life of Fénelon at the expense of the other. What magic is there in the pronoun 'my' that should justify us in overturning the decisions of impartial truth? My brother or my father may be a fool or a profligate, malicious, lying or dishonest. If they be, of what consequence is it that they are mine? . . .

Thus every view of the subject brings us back to the consideration of my neighbour's moral worth, and his importance to the general weal, as the only standard to determine the treatment to which he is entitled. Gratitude therefore, if by gratitude we understand a sentiment of preference which I entertain towards another, upon the ground of my having been the subject of his benefits, is no part either of justice or virtue. . . .

The soundest criterion of virtue is to put ourselves in the place of an impartial spectator, of an angelic nature, suppose, beholding us from an elevated station, and uninfluenced by our prejudices, conceiving what would be his estimate of the intrinsic circumstances of our neighbour, and acting accordingly.

Having considered the persons with whom justice is conversant, let us next enquire into the degree in which we are obliged to consult the good of others. And here, upon the very same reasons, it will follow that it is just I should do all the good in my power. Does a person in distress apply to me for relief? It is my duty to grant it, and I commit a breach of duty in refusing. If this principle be not of universal application, it is because, in conferring a benefit upon an individual, I may in some instances inflict an injury of superior magnitude upon myself or society. Now the same justice that binds me to any individual of my fellow men binds me to the whole. If, while I confer a benefit upon one man, it appear, in striking an equitable balance, that I am injuring the whole, my action ceases to be right, and becomes absolutely wrong. But how much am I bound to do for the general weal, that is, for the benefit of the individuals of whom the whole is composed? Everything in my power. To the neglect of the means of my own existence? No; for I am myself a part of the whole. Beside, it will rarely happen that the project of doing for others everything in my power will not demand for its execution the preservation of my own existence; or in other words, it will rarely happen that I cannot do more good in twenty years than in one. If the extraordinary case should occur in which I can promote the general good by my death more than by my life, justice requires that I should be content to die. In other cases, it will usually be incumbent on me to maintain my body and mind in the utmost vigour, and in the best condition for service.[10]

4 Private and Domestic Affections

Virtue is nothing else but kind and sympathetic feelings reduced into principle. Undisciplined feeling would induce me, now to interest myself exclusively for one man, and now for another, to be eagerly solicitous for those who are present to me, and to forget the absent. Feeling ripened into virtue embraces the interests of the whole human race, and constantly proposes to itself the production of the greatest quantity of happiness. But, while it anxiously adjusts the balance of interests, and yields to no case, however urgent, to the prejudice of the whole, it keeps aloof from the unmeaning rant of romance, and uniformly recollects that happiness, in order to be real, must necessarily be individual.[11]

---

10 *P.J.*, Bk. II, ch. ii.
11 *P.J.*, Bk. V, ch. xvi.

There seems to be more truth in the argument, derived chiefly from the prevailing modes of social existence, in favour of my providing, in ordinary cases, for my wife and children, my brothers and relations, before I provide for strangers, than in those which have just been examined. As long as the providing for individuals is conducted with its present irregularity and caprice, it seems as if there must be a certain distribution of the class needing superintendence and supply, among the class affording it; that each man may have his claim and resource. But this argument is to be admitted with great caution. It belongs only to ordinary cases; and cases of a higher order, or a more urgent necessity, will perpetually occur in competition with which these will be altogether impotent.[12]

I apprehend domestic and private affections inseparable from the nature of man, and from what may be styled the culture of the heart, and am fully persuaded that they are not incompatible with a profound and active sense of justice in the mind of him that cherishes them. The way in which these seemingly jarring principles may be reconciled, is in part pointed out in a recent publication of mine *Memoirs of the Author of a Vindication of the Rights of Woman,* the words of which I will here therefore take the liberty to repeat. They are these:

A sound morality requires that *nothing human should be regarded by us as indifferent;* but it is impossible we should not feel the strongest interest for those persons whom we know most intimately, and whose welfare and sympathies are united to our own. True wisdom will recommend to us individual attachments; for with them our minds are more thoroughly maintained in activity and life than they can be under the privation of them, and it is better that man should be a living being, than a stock or a stone. True virtue will sanction this recommendation; since it is the object of virtue to produce happiness; and since the man who lives in the midst of domestic relations, will have many opportunities of conferring pleasure, minute in the detail, yet not trivial in the amount, without interfering with the purposes of general benevolence. Nay, by kindling his sensibility, and harmonising his soul, they may be expected,

---

12 *P.J.*, Bk. II, ch. ii.

if he is endowed with a liberal and manly spirit, to render him more prompt in the service of strangers and the public.[13]

The idea of justice there contained [in *Political Justice*] is, that it is a rule requiring from us such an application of 'our talents, our understanding, our strength and our time', as shall, in the result, produce the greatest sum of pleasure, to the sum of those beings who are capable of enjoying the sensation of pleasure.—Now, if I divide my time into portions, and consider how the majority of the smaller portions may be so employed, as most effectually to procure pleasure to others, nothing is more obvious, than that many of these portions cannot be employed so effectually in procuring pleasure, as to my immediate connections and familiars: he therefore who would be the best moral economist of his time, must employ much of it in seeking the advantage and content of those, with whom he has most frequent intercourse. Accordingly it is there maintained, that the external action recommended by this, and by the commonly received systems of morality, will in the generality of cases be the same, all the difference lying in this, that the motives exciting to action, upon the one principle, and the other, will be essentially different.

Here, according to my present admission, lies all the error of which I am conscious, in the original statement in the *Enquiry concerning Political Justice*: I would now say that, 'in the generality of cases', not only the external action, but the motive, ought to be nearly the same as in the commonly received systems of morality; that I ought not only, 'in ordinary cases, to provide for my wife and children, my brothers and relations, before I provide for strangers', (p. 67) but that it would be well that my doing so, should arise from the operation of those private and domestic affections, by which through all ages of the world the conduct of mankind has been excited and directed.[14]

The human mind is so constituted, as to render our actions in almost every case much more the creatures of sentiment and affection, than of the understanding. We all of us have, twisted with our very natures, the principles of parental and filial affection, of love, attachment and

---

13 *Memoirs of the Author of a Vindication of the Rights of Woman*, 2nd ed., 90–91.
14 *Thoughts*, 27–28.

friendship. I do therefore not think it the primordial duty of the moralist to draw forth all the powers of his wit in the recommendation of these.

Parental and filial affection, and the sentiments of love, attachment and friendship, are most admirable instruments in the execution of the purposes of virtue. But to each of them, in the great chart of a just moral conduct, must be assigned its sphere. They are all liable to excess. Each must be kept within its bounds, and have rigorous limits assigned it. I must take care not so to love, or so to obey my love to my parent or child, as to intrench upon an important and paramount public good.[15]

He who forever thinks, that his 'charity must begin at home', is in great danger of becoming an indifferent citizen, and of withering those feelings of philanthropy, which in all sound estimation constitute the crowning glory of man. He will perhaps have a reasonable affection towards what he calls his own flesh and blood, and may assist even a stranger in a case of urgent distress.—But it is dangerous to trifle with the first principles and sentiments of morality. And this man will scarcely in any case have his mind prepared to hail the first dawnings of human improvement, and to regard all that belongs to the welfare of his kind as parcel of his own particular estate.[16]

5 Benevolence

When we have entered into so auspicious a path as that of disinterestedness, reflection confirms our choice, in a sense in which it never can confirm any of the factitious passions we have named. We find by observation that we are surrounded by beings of the same nature with ourselves. They have the same senses, are susceptible of the same pleasures and pains, capable of being raised to the same excellence and employed in the same usefulness. We are able in imagination to go out of ourselves, and become impartial spectators of the system of which we are a part. We can then make an estimate of our intrinsic and absolute value; and detect the imposition of that self-regard which would represent our own interest as of as much value as that of all the world besides.[17]

---

15 *Thoughts*, 31–32.
16 *T.M.*, 222.
17 *P.J.*, Bk. IV, ch. x.

Study is cold, if it not be enlivened with the idea of the happiness to arise to mankind from the cultivation and improvement of sciences. The sublime and pathetic are barren, unless it be the sublime of true virtue, and the pathos of true sympathy. The pleasures of the mere man of taste and refinement, 'play round the head, but come not to the heart'. There is no true joy but in the spectacle and contemplation of happiness. There is no delightful melancholy but in pitying distress. The man who has once performed an act of exalted generosity knows that there is no sensation of corporeal or intellectual taste to be compared with this. The man who has sought to benefit nations rises above the mechanical ideas of barter and exchange. He asks no gratitude. To see that they are benefited, or to believe that they will be so, is its own reward. He ascends to the highest of human pleasures, the pleasures of disinterestedness. He enjoys all the good that mankind possess, and all the good that he perceives to be in reserve for them. No man so truly promotes his own interest as he that forgets it. No man reaps so copious a harvest of pleasure as he who thinks only of the pleasures of other men.[18]

6 Duty

There are two subjects of the utmost importance to a just delineation of the principles of society, which are, on that account, entitled to a separate examination: the duties incumbent on men living in society, and the rights accruing to them. These are merely different modes of expressing the principle of justice, as it shall happen to be considered in its relation to the agent or the patient. Duty is the treatment I am bound to bestow upon others; right is the treatment I am entitled to expect from them. . . .

I would define virtue to be any action or actions of an intelligent being proceeding from kind and benevolent intention and having a tendency to contribute to general happiness. . . . Intention no doubt is of the essence of virtue. But it will not do alone. In deciding the merits of others, we are bound, for the most part, to proceed in the same manner as in deciding the merits of inanimate substances. The turning point is their utility. Intention is of no further value than as it leads to utility: it is the means, and not the end. . . .

Duty is that mode of action on the part of the individual which constitutes the best possible application of his capacity to the general

---

18 *P.J.*, Bk. IV, ch. xi.

benefit. The only distinction to be made between what was there and adduced upon the subject of personal virtue, and the observations which most aptly apply to the considerations of duty, consists in this: that, though a man should in some instances neglect the best application of his capacity, he may yet be entitled to the appellation of virtuous; but duty is uniform, and requires of us that best application in every situation that presents itself.[19]

There are two circumstances required, to entitle an action to be denominated virtuous. It must have a tendency to produce good rather than evil to the race of man, and it must have been generated by an intention to produce such good. The most beneficent action that ever was performed, if it did not spring from the intention of good to others, is not of the nature of virtue. Virtue, where it exists in any eminence, is a species of conduct, modelled upon a true estimate of the good intended to be produced. He that makes a false estimate, and prefers a trivial and partial good to an important and comprehensive one, is vicious.[20]

7 Rights

The real or supposed rights of man are two kinds, active and passive; the right in certain cases to do as we list; and the right we possess to the forbearance or assistance of other men.

The first of these a just philosophy will probably induce us to universally explode.

There is no sphere in which a human being can be supposed to act where one mode of proceeding will not, in every given instance, be more reasonable than any other mode. That mode the being is bound by every principle of justice to pursue. . . . There is not one of our avocations or amusements that does not, by its effects, render us more or less fit to contribute our quota to the general utility. If then everyone of our actions fall within the province of morals, it follows that we have no rights in relation to the selecting them. No one will maintain that we have a right to trespass upon the dictates of morality. . . .

[Man] is said to have a right to life and personal liberty. This proposition, if admitted, must be admitted with great limitation. He has no

---

19 *P.J.*, Bk. II, ch. iv.
20 *T.M.*, 209.

71

right to his life when his duty calls him to resign it. Other men are bound (it would be improper in strictness of speech, upon the ground of the preceding explanations, to say they have a right) to deprive him of life and liberty, if that should appear in any case to be indispensably necessary to prevent a greater evil. The passive rights of man will be best understood from the following elucidation.

Every man has a certain sphere of discretion which he has a right to expect shall not be infringed by his neighbours. This right flows from the very nature of man. First, all men are fallible: no man can be justified in setting up his judgment as a standard for others. We have no infallible judge of controversies; each man in his own apprehension is right in his decisions; and we can find no satisfactory mode of adjusting their jarring pretensions. If everyone be desirous of imposing his sense upon others, it will at last come to be a controversy, not of reason, but of force. Secondly, even if we had an infallible criterion, nothing would be gained, unless it were by all men recognized as such. If I were secured against the possibility of mistake, mischief and not good would accrue, from imposing my infallible truths upon my neighbour, and requiring his submission independently of any conviction I could produce in his understanding. Man is a being who can never be an object of just approbation, any further than he is independent. He must consult his own reason, draw his own conclusions and conscientiously conform himself to his ideas of propriety. Without this, he will be neither active, nor considerate, nor resolute, nor generous. For these two reasons it is necessary that every man should stand by himself, and rest upon his own understanding. For that purpose each must have his sphere of discretion. No man must encroach upon my province, nor I upon his. He may advise me, moderately and without pertinaciousness, but he must not expect to dictate to me. He may censure me freely and without reserve; but he should remember that I am to act by my deliberation and not his. He may exercise a republican boldness in judging, but he must not be peremptory and imperious in prescribing. Force may never be resorted to but in the most extraordinary and imperious emergency. I ought to exercise my talents for the benefit of others; but that exercise must be the fruit of my own conviction; no man must attempt to press me into the service. I ought to appropriate such part of the fruits of the earth as by any accident comes into my possession, and is not necessary to my benefit, to the use of others; but they must obtain it from me by argument and expostulation, not by violence.

It is in this principle that what is commonly called the right of property is founded. Whatever then comes into my possession, without violence to any other man, or to the institution of society, is my property. This property, it appears by the principles already laid down, I have no right to dispose of at my caprice; every shilling of it is appropriated by the laws of morality; but no man can be justified, in ordinary cases at least, in forcibly extorting it from me. When the laws of morality shall be clearly understood, their excellence is universally apprehended, and themselves seen to be coincident with each man's private advantage, the idea of property in this sense will remain, but no man will have the least desire, for purposes of ostentation or luxury, to possess more than his neighbours.

A second branch of the passive rights of man consists in the right each man possesses to the assistance of his neighbour.[21]

In every moral question, or in other words, in every question where the pleasure or pain, the happiness or unhappiness of others is concerned, there is one thing that it is a man's duty to do, and he has no right to do otherwise.

The rich man therefore has no right to withhold his assistance from his brother-man in distress, except in the sense that he cannot reasonably be brought under the jurisdiction of a court of justice, for his breach of the moral law in this respect.

The rights of any man as to his treatment of his fellow-man, are rights of discretion merely: in other words, that no man must attempt to compel him to do, that which is his duty to do. The appeal is exclusively to the judgment of him who is to act; but he is bound to inform his judgment to the utmost of his power, and rigorously to adhere to the unbiased decisions of that judgment. So far is it from being true, that 'every man has a right to do what he will with his own'.[22]

8 Coercion

Coercion cannot convince, cannot conciliate, but on the contrary alienates the mind of him against whom it is employed. Coercion has nothing in common with reason, and herefore can have no proper tendency to the cultivation of virtue. It is true that reason is nothing more than a

---

21 *P.J.*, Bk. II, ch. v.
22 *Of Population*, 545–46.

collation and comparison of various emotions and feelings; but they must be feelings originally appropriate to the question, not those which an arbitrary will, stimulated by the possession of power, may annex to it. Reason is omnipotent: if my conduct be wrong, a very simple statement, flowing from a clear and comprehensive view, will make it appear to be such; nor is it probable that there is any perverseness that would persist in vice in the face of all the recommendations with which virtue might be invested, and all the beauty in which it might be displayed.[23]

The argument against political coercion is equally strong against the infliction of private penalties, between master and slave, and between parent and child. There was, in reality, not only more gallantry, but more of reason in the Gothic system of trial by duel than in these. The trial of force is over in these, as we have already said, before the exertion of force is begun. All that remains is the leisurely infliction of torture, my power to inflict it being placed in my joints and sinews. This whole argument seems liable to an irresistible dilemma. The right of the parent over his offspring lies either in his superior strength, or his superior reason. If in his strength, we have only to apply this right universally in order to drive morality out of the world. If in his reason, in that reason let him confide. It is a poor argument of my superior reason that I am unable to make justice be apprehended and felt, in the most necessary cases, without the intervention of blows.

Let us consider the effect that coercion produces upon the mind of him against whom it is employed. It cannot begin with convincing; it is no argument. It begins with producing the sensation of pain, and the sentiment of distaste. It begins with violently alienating the mind from the truth with which we wish it to be impressed. It includes in it a tacit confession of imbecility. If he who employs coercion against me could mould me to his purposes by argument, no doubt he would. He pretends to punish me because his argument is strong; but he really punishes me because his argument is weak.[24]

Man is an intellectual being. There is no way to make him virtuous but in calling forth his intellectual powers. There is no way to make him

23 *P.J.*, Bk. VII, ch. iii.
24 *P.J.*, Bk. VII, ch. ii.

virtuous but by making him independent. He must study the laws of nature, and the necessary consequences of actions, not the arbitrary caprice of his superior. Do you desire that I should work? Do not drive me to it with the whip; for, if, before I thought it better to be idle, this will but increase my alienation. Persuade my understanding, and render it the subject of my choice. It can only be by the most deplorable perversion of reason that we can be induced to believe any species of slavery, from the slavery of the school-boy to that of the most unfortunate Negro in our West India plantations, favourable to virtue.[25]

9 Promises

When I enter into an engagement, I engage for that which is in its own nature conducive to human happiness, or which is not so. Can my engagement always render that which before was injurious agreeable to, and that which was beneficial the opposite of duty? Previously to my entering into a promise, there is something which I ought to promise, and something which I ought not. Previously to my entering into a promise, all modes of action were not indifferent. Nay, the very opposite of this is true. Every conceivable mode of action has its appropriate tendency, and shade of tendency, to benefit or to mischief, and consequently its appropriate claim to be performed or avoided. Thus clearly does it appear that promises and compacts are not the foundation of morality.

Secondly, I observe that promises are, absolutely considered, an evil, and stand in opposition to the genuine and wholesome exercise of an intellectual nature. . . .

These principles are calculated to set in a clearer light than they have often been exhibited, the cases that authorise the violation of promises. Compact is not the foundation of morality; on the contrary, it is an expedient to which we are sometimes obliged to have resort, but the introduction of which must always be regarded by an enlightened observer with jealousy. It ought never to be called forth but in cases of the clearest necessity. It is not the principle upon which our common happiness reposes; it is only one of the means for securing that happiness. The adherence to promises therefore, as well as their employment in the first instance, must be decided by the general criterion, and

---

25 *P.J.*, Bk. VII, ch. vi.

maintained only so far as, upon a comprehensive view, it shall be found productive of a balance of happiness. . . .

Few things can be more absurd than to talk of our having promised obedience to the laws. If the laws depend upon promises for their execution, why are they accompanied by sanctions? Why is it considered as the great arcanum of legislation to make laws that are easy of execution, and that need no assistance from the execrable intervention of oaths and informers? Again, why should I promise that I will do everything that a certain power, called the government, shall imagine it convenient, or decide that it is fitting, for me to do? Is there in this either morality, or justice, or common sense? Does brute force alone communicate to its possessor a sufficient claim upon my veneration? For, be it observed, the wisdom or duty of obedience proceeds upon exactly the same principle, whether it be to a tyrant, or to the most regularly elected house of representatives. There is but one power to which I can yield a heart-felt obedience, the decision of my own understanding, the dictate of my own conscience. The decrees of any other power, especially if I have a firm and independent mind, I shall obey with reluctance and aversion. My obedience is purely an affair of composition: I choose to do that which, in itself considered, my judgement disapproves, rather than incur the greater evil which the power from whom the mandate issues annexes to my disobedience.[26]

10 Marriage

[The] subject of cohabitation is particularly interesting, as it includes in it the subject of marriage. . . . Cohabitation is not only an evil as it checks the independent progress of mind; it is also inconsistent with the imperfections and propensities of man. It is absurd to expect the inclinations and wishes of two human beings should coincide through any long period of time. To oblige them to act and live together, is to subject them to some inevitable portion of thwarting, bickering and unhappiness. This cannot be otherwise, so long as man has failed to reach the standard of absolute perfection. The supposition that I must have a companion for life, is the result of a complication of vices. It is the dictate of cowardice, not of fortitude. It flows from the desire of being loved and esteemed for something other that is not desert.

---

26 *P.J.*, Bk. III, ch. iii.

But the evil of marriage as it is practised in European countries lies deeper than this. The habit is, for a thoughtless and romantic youth of each sex to come together, to see each other for a few times and under circumstances full of delusion, and then to vow to each other eternal attachment. What is the consequence of this? In almost every instance they find themselves deceived. They are reduced to make the best of an irretrievable mistake. They are presented with the strongest imaginable temptation to become the dupe of falsehood. They are led to conceive it their wisest policy to shut their eyes upon realities, happy if by any perversion of intellect they can persuade themselves that they were right in their first crude opinion of each other. The institution of marriage is a system of fraud; and men who carefully mislead their judgements in the daily affair of their life, must have a crippled judgement in every other concern.

We ought to dismiss our mistake as soon as it is detected; but we are taught to cherish it. We ought to be incessant in our search after virtue and worth; but we are taught to check our enquiry, and shut our eyes upon the most attractive and admirable objects. Marriage is law, and the worst of all laws. Whatever our understandings may tell us of the person from whose connection we should derive the greatest improvement, of the worth of one woman and the demerits of another, we are obliged to consider what is law, not what is justice.

Add to this, that marriage is an affair of property, and the worst of all properties. So long as two human beings are forbidden by positive institution to follow the dictates of their own mind, prejudice is alive and vigorous. So long as I seek to engross one woman to myself, and to prohibit my neighbour from proving his superior desert and reaping the fruits of it, I am guilty of the most odious of all monopolies. Over this imaginary prize men watch with perpetual jealousy, and one man will find his desires and his capacity to circumvent as much excited, as the other is excited to traverse his projects and frustrate his hopes. As long as this state of society continues, philanthropy will be crossed and checked in a thousand ways, and the still augmenting stream of abuse will continue to flow.

The abolition of marriage will be attended with no evils. We are apt to represent it to ourselves as the harbinger of brutal lust and depravity. But what really happens in this as in other cases, that the positive laws which are made to restrain our vices, irritate and multiply them. Not to say, that the same sentiments of justice and happiness which in a state of equal property would destroy the relish for luxury, would decrease our inordinate appetites of every kind, and lead us universally to prefer the pleasures of intellect to the pleasures of sense.

The intercourse of the sexes will in such a state fall under the same system as any other species of friendship. Exclusively of all groundless and obstinate attachments, it will be impossible for me to live in the world without finding one man of worth superior to that of any other whom I have an opportunity of observing. To this man I shall feel a kindness in exact proportion to my apprehension of his worth. The case will be precisely the same with respect to the female sex. I shall assiduously cultivate the intercourse of that woman whose accomplishments shall strike me in the most powerful manner. 'But it may happen that other men will feel for her the same preference that I do.' This will create no difficulty. We may all enjoy her conversation; and we shall all be wise enough to consider the sensual intercourse as a very trivial object. This, like every other affair in which two persons are concerned, must be regulated in each successive instance by the unforced consent of either party. . . .

Such are some of the considerations that will probably regulate the commerce of the sexes. It cannot be definitively affirmed whether it be known in such a state of society who is the father of each individual child. But it may be affirmed that such knowledge will be of no importance. It is aristocracy, self love and family pride that teach us to set a value upon it at present. I ought to prefer no human being to another, because that being my father, my wife or my son, but because, for reasons which equally appeal to all understandings, that being is entitled to preference. One among the measures which will successively be dictated by the spirit of democracy, and that probably at no great distance, is the abolition of surnames.[27]

11 Religion

All that can be told me of a future world, a world of spirits, or of glorified bodies, where the employments are spiritual, and the first cause is to be rendered a subject of immediate perception, or of a scene of retribution, where the mind, doomed to everlasting inactivity, shall be

---

27 *P.J.* (1793) Bk. VIII, ch. vi.

wholly a prey to the upbraidings of remorse, and the sarcasms of devils, is so foreign to everything with which I am acquainted, that my mind in vain endeavours to believe or understand it. If doctrines like these occupy the habitual reflections of any, it is not of the lawless, the violent and ungovernable, but of the sober and conscientious, overwhelming them with gratuitous anxiety, or persuading them passively to submit to despotism and injustice, that they may receive the recompense of their patience hereafter. This objection is equally applicable to every species of deception. Fables may amuse the imagination; but can never stand in the place of reason and judgment as the principles of human conduct.[28]

Such are the effects that a code of religious conformity produces upon a clergy; let us consider the effects that are produced upon their country-men. They are bid to look for instruction and morality to a denomina-tion of men, formal, embarrassed and hypocritical, in whom the main spring of intellect is unbent and incapable of action. If the people be not blinded with religious zeal, they will discover and despise the imperfec-tions of their spiritual guides. If they be so blinded, they will not the less transplant into their own characters the imbecile and unworthy spirit they are not able to detect. Is virtue so deficient in attractions, as to be incapable of gaining adherents to her standard? Far otherwise. Nothing can bring the wisdom of a just and pure conduct into question but the circumstance of its being recommended to us from an equivocal quarter. The most malicious enemy of mankind could not have invented a scheme more destructive of their true happiness than that of hiring, at the expense of the state, a body of men whose business it should seem to be to dupe their contemporaries into the practice of virtue.[29]

If public worship be conformable to reason, reason without doubt will prove adequate to its vindication and support. If it be from God, it is profanation to imagine that it stands in need of the alliance of the state. It must be, in an eminent degree, artificial and exotic, if it be incapable of preserving itself in existence otherwise than by the inauspicious interference of political institution.[30]

---

28 *P.J.*, Bk. V, ch. v.
29 *P.J.*, Bk. VI, ch. ii.
30 *P.J.*, Bk. VI, ch. ii.

The doctrine of the injustice of accumulated property has been the foundation of all religious morality. Its most energetic teachers have been irresistibly led to assert the precise truth in this respect. They have taught the rich that they hold their wealth only as a trust, that they are strictly accountable for every atom of their expenditure, that they are merely administrators, and by no means proprietors in chief. But, while religion thus inculcated on mankind the pure principles of justice, the majority of its professors have been but too apt to treat the practice of justice, not as a debt, which it ought to be considered, but as an affair of spontaneous generosity and bounty.[31]

Religion was the generous ebullition of men who let their imagination loose on the grandest of subjects, and wandered without restraint in the unbounded field of enquiry. It is not to be wondered at therefore if they brought home imperfect ideas of the sublimest views that intellect can furnish.[32]

There is nothing perhaps that has contributed more to the introduction and perpetuating of bigotry in the world, than the doctrines of the Christian religion. It caused the spirit of intolerance to strike a deeper root; and it has entailed that spirit upon many who have shaken off the directer influence of its tenets. It is the characteristic of this religion, to lay the utmost stress upon faith. Its central doctrine is contained in this short maxim, He that believeth, shall be saved; and he that believeth not, shall be damned.[33]

The circumstances of every day tend to confirm in him [the clergyman] a dogmatical, imperious, illiberal and intolerant character.

Such are the leading features of the character which, in most instances, we must expect to find in a reputable clergyman. He will be timid in enquiry, prejudiced in opinion, cold, formal, the slave of what other men may think of him, rude, dictatorial, impatient of contradiction, harsh in his censures, and illiberal in his judgments. Every man may

---

31 *P.J.*, Bk. VIII, ch. i.
32 *P.J.*, Bk. VIII, ch. iii.
33 William Godwin, *The Enquirer* (Edinburgh: John Anderson, 1797), 522–23.

remark in him study rendered abortive, artificial manners, infantine prejudices, and a sort of arrogant infallibility.[34]

Christianity is, and has always been called, a religion of charity and love. It is rigorous in prescribing the duties of the rich, as well as of the poor. It does not admit that we 'have a right to do what we will with our own'. On the contrary, it teaches that we have nothing that we can strictly call our own, that the rich are but stewards and administrators of the benefits of Providence, and that we shall be austerely called to give an account of every talent that is entrusted to us. We are taught to consider our fellow-creatures in distress as our brothers, and to treat them accordingly. 'Inasmuch as ye have done it to one of the least of these, ye have done it to me.'[35]

---

34 Ibid., 232.
35 *Of Population*, 623.

IV

POLITICS

1 Political Enquiry

Political enquiry may be distributed under two heads: first, what are the regulations which will conduce to the well being of man in society; and, secondly, what is the authority which is competent to prescribe regulations.

The regulations to which the conduct of men living in society ought to be conformed may be considered in two ways: first, those moral laws which are enjoined upon us by the dictates of enlightened reason; and, secondly, those principles a deviation from which the interest of the community may be supposed to render it proper to repress by sanctions and punishment.[1]

The great problem of political knowledge is, how to preserve to mankind the advantages of freedom, together with an authority strong enough to control every daring violation of general security and peace. The prize of political wisdom is due to the man who shall afford us the best comment upon that fundamental principle of civilization, Liberty without Licentiousness.[2]

Politics is nothing else, but one chapter extracted out of the great code of morality. While therefore the criterion of virtue remains unchanged, the conduct which ought to be held by states, by governments and subjects, and the principles of judicial proceeding between man and man will remain forever the same. In the *Enquiry concerning Political Justice* it

---

1   *P.J.*, Bk. II, ch. i.
2   William Godwin, *Considerations on Lord Grenville's and Mr. Pitt's Bills* (London: J. Johnson, 1795), 2.

is endeavoured to be proved, that in morality each man is entitled to a certain sphere for the exercise of his discretion; that it is to be desired that in this sphere he should be directed by a free, and instructed and independent judgment; and that it is necessary for the improvement of mankind that no man or body of men should entrench upon this sphere but in cases of the most irresistible urgency. The inference drawn from these particulars is, that the less government we had, and the fewer were the instances in which government interfered with the proceedings of individuals, consistently with the preservation of the social state, the better would it prove for the welfare and happiness of man.[3]

2 Government

Society is no more than an aggregation of individuals. Its claims and duties must be the aggregate of their claims and duties, the one no more precarious and arbitrary than the other. What has the society a right to require from me? The question is already answered: everything that it is my duty to do. Anything more? Certainly not.[4]

Man associated at first for the sake of mutual assistance. They did not foresee any mutual restraint would be necessary to regulate the conduct of individual members of the society towards each other, or towards the whole. The necessity grew out of the errors and perverseness of a few. An acute writer [Thomas Paine] has expressed this idea with peculiar felicity. 'Society and government', says he, 'are different in themselves, and have different origins. Society is produced by our wants, and government by our wickedness. Society is in every state a blessing; government even in its best state but a necessary evil.'[5]

The rich are in all such countries directly or indirectly the legislators of the state; and of consequence are perpetually reducing oppression into a system, and depriving the poor of that little commonage of nature which might otherwise still have remained to them.[6]

---

3   *Thoughts*, 49.
4   *P.J.*, Bk. II, ch. ii.
5   *P.J.*, Bk. II, ch. i.
6   *P.J.*, Bk. I, ch. iii.

All government is founded in opinion. Men at present live under any particular form because they conceive it their interest to do so. One part indeed of a community or empire may be held in subjugation by force; but this cannot be the personal force of a despot; it must be the force of another part of the community, who are of the opinion that it is their interest to support his authority. Destroy this opinion, and the fabric which is built upon it falls to the ground. It follows therefore that all men are essentially independent.[7]

Government, under whatever point of view we examine this topic, is unfortunately pregnant with motives to censure and complaint. Incessant change, everlasting innovation, seem to be dictated by the true interests of mankind. But government is the perpetual enemy of change. What was admirably observed of a particular system of government is in a great degree true of all: They 'lay their hand on the spring there is in society, and put a stop to its motion'. Their tendency is to perpetuate abuse. Whatever was once thought right and useful they undertake to entail to the latest posterity. They reverse the genuine propensities of man, and, instead of suffering us to proceed, teach us to look backward for perfection. They prompt us to seek the public welfare, not in alteration and improvement, but in a timid reverence for the decisions of our ancestors, as if it were the nature of the human mind always to degenerate, and never to advance.

Man is in a state of perpetual mutation. He must grow either better or worse, either correct his habits or confirm them. The government under which we are placed must either increase our passions and prejudices by fanning the flame, or, by gradually discouraging, tend to extirpate them. In reality, it is impossible to conceive a government that shall have the latter tendency. By its very nature positive institution has a tendency to suspend the elasticity and progress of mind. Every scheme for embodying perfection must be injurious. That which is today a considerable melioration will at some future period, if preserved unaltered, appear a defect and disease in the body politic. It is earnestly to be desired that each man should be wise enough to govern himself, without the intervention of any compulsory restraint; and since government, even in its best state, is an evil, the object principally to be aimed

---

7   *P.J.*, Bk. II, ch. iii.

at is that we should have as little of it as the general peace of human society will permit.[8]

Government is little capable of affording benefit of the first importance to mankind. It is calculated to induce us to lament, not the apathy and indifference, but the inauspicious activity of government. It incites us to look for the moral improvement of the species, not in the multiplying of regulations, but in their repeal. It teaches us that truth and virtue, like commerce, will then flourish most when least subjected to the mistaken guardianship of authority and laws. This maxim will rise upon us in its importance in proportion as we connect it with the numerous departments of political justice to which it will be found to have relation. As fast as it shall be adopted into the practice of mankind, it may be expected to deliver us from a weight, intolerable to mind, and, in the highest degree, hostile to the progress of truth.[9]

Government cannot proceed but upon confidence, as confidence on the other hand cannot exist without ignorance. The true supporters of government are the weak and uninformed, and not the wise. In proportion as weakness and ignorance shall diminish, the basis of government will also decay. This however is an event which ought not to be contemplated with alarm. A catastrophe of this description would be the true euthanasia of government. If the annihilation of blind confidence and implicit opinion can at any time be effected, there will necessarily succeed in their place an unforced concurrence of all in promoting the general welfare.[10]

The true reason why the mass of mankind has so often been made the dupe of knaves has been the mysterious and complicated nature of the social system. Once annihilate the quackery of government, and the most homebred understanding might be strong enough to detect the artifices of the state juggler that would mislead him.[11]

---

8   *P.J.*, Bk. III, ch. vii.
9   *P.J.*, Bk. VI, ch. i.
10   *P.J.*, Bk. III, ch. vi.
11   *P.J.*, Bk. V, ch. xxiii.

With what delight must every well informed friend of mankind look forward to the auspicious period, the dissolution of political government, of that brute engine which has been the only perennial cause of the vices of mankind, and which, as has abundantly appeared in the progress of the present work, has mischiefs of various sorts incorporated with its substance, and no otherwise removable than by its utter annihilation![12]

3 Social Contract

If government be founded in the consent of the people, it can have no power over any individual by whom that consent is refused. If a tacit consent be not sufficient, still less can I be deemed to have consented to a measure upon which I put an express negative. This immediately follows from the observations of Rousseau. If the people, or the individuals of whom the people is constituted, cannot delegate their authority to a representative, neither can any individual delegate his authority to a majority, in an assembly of which he himself is a member. That must surely be a singular species of consent the external indications of which are often to be found in an unremitting opposition in the first instance, and the compulsory subjection in the second.[13]

If you demand my assent to any proposition, it is necessary that the proposition should be stated simply and clearly. So numerous are the varieties of human understanding, in all cases where its independence and integrity are sufficiently preserved, that there is little chance of any two men coming to a precise agreement about ten successive propositions that are in their own nature open to debate. What then can be more absurd than to present to me the laws of England in fifty volumes folio, and call upon me to give an honest and uninfluenced vote upon their contents?[14]

4 Constitutions

Either a people must be governed according to their own apprehensions of justice and truth, or they must not. The last of these assertions cannot be avowed, but upon the unequivocal principles of tyranny. But,

---

12 *P.J.*, Bk. V, ch. xxiv.
13 *P.J.*, Bk. III, ch. ii.
14 *P.J.*, Bk. III, ch. ii.

if the first be true, then it is just as absurd to say to a nation, 'This government, which you chose nine years ago, is the legitimate government, and the government which your present sentiments approve, the illegitimate'; as to insist upon their being governed by the *dicta* of their remotest ancestors, even of their most insolent usurper. . . .

The distinction of constitutional and ordinary topics will always appear in practice unintelligible and vexatious by the apprehension that they shall invade the constitution. In a country where the people are habituated to sentiments of equality, and where no political monopoly is tolerated, there is little danger that any national assembly should be disposed to enforce a pernicious change, and there is still less that the people should submit to the injury, or not possess the means easily and with small interruption of public tranquillity, to avert it. The language of reason on this subject is, 'Give us equality and justice, but no constitution. Suffer us to follow, without restraint, the dictates of our own judgment, and to change our forms of social order, as fast as we improve in understanding and knowledge.'[15]

5 Legislation

Legislation, as it has been usually understood, is not an affair of human competence. Immutable reason is the true legislator, and her decrees it behoves us to investigate. The functions of society extend, not to the making, but the interpreting of law; it cannot decree, it can only declare that which the nature of things has already decreed, and the propriety of which irresistibly flows from the circumstances of the case.[16]

Legislation has already appeared to be a term not applicable to human society. Men cannot do more than declare and interpret law; nor can there be an authority so paramount as to have the prerogative of making that to be law which abstract and immutable justice had not made to be law previously to that interposition.[17]

Legislation, that is, the authoritative enunciation of abstract or general propositions, is a function of equivocal nature, and will never be

---

15 *P.J.*, Bk. VI, ch. vii.
16 *P.J.*, Bk. III, ch. v.
17 *P.J.*, Bk. V, ch. i.

exercised in a pure state of society, or a state approaching to purity, but with great caution and unwillingness. It is the most absolute of the functions of government, and government itself is a remedy that inevitably brings its own evils along with it. Administration, on the other hand, is a principle of perpetual application. So long as men shall see reason to act in a corporate capacity, they will always have occasions of temporary emergency for which to provide. In proportion as they advance in social improvement, executive power will, comparatively speaking, become everything, and legislative nothing.[18]

6 Law

If a society be contented with the rules of justice, and do not assume to itself the right of distorting or adding to those rules, there law is evidently a less necessary institution. The rules of justice would be more clearly and effectively taught by an actual intercourse with human society, unrestrained by the fetters of prepossession, than they can be by catechisms and codes.

One result of the institution of law is that the institution, once begun, can never be brought to a close. Edict is heaped upon edict, and volume upon volume. This will be most the case where the government is most popular, and its proceedings have most in them of the nature of deliberation. Surely this is no slight indication that the principle is wrong, and that, of consequence, the further we proceed in the path it marks out to us, the more we shall be bewildered. . . .

There is no maxim more clear than this, 'Every case is a rule to itself.' No action of any man was ever the same as any other action, had ever the same degree of utility or injury. It should seem to be the business of justice to distinguish the qualities of men, and not, which has hitherto been the practice, to confound them. But what has been the result of an attempt to do this in relation to law? As new cases occur, the law is perpetually found deficient. How should it be otherwise? Lawgivers have not the faculty of unlimited prescience, and cannot define that which is boundless. The alternative that remains is either to wrest the law to include a case which was never in the contemplation of its authors, or to make a new law to provide for this particular case. Much has been done in the first of these modes. The quibbles of lawyers,

---

18 *P.J.*, Bk. V, ch. xxi.

and the arts by which they refine and distort the sense of the law, are proverbial. But, though much is done, everything cannot be thus done. The abuse will sometimes be too palpable. Not to say that the very education that enables the lawyer, when he is employed for the prosecutor, to find out offences the lawgiver never meant, enables him, when he is employed for the defendant, to discover subterfuges that reduce the law to nullity. It is therefore perpetually necessary to make new laws. These laws, in order to escape evasion, are frequently tedious, minute and circumlocutory. The volume in which justice records her prescriptions is for ever increasing, and the world would not contain the books that might be written.

The consequence of the infinitude of law is its uncertainty. This strikes at the principle upon which law is founded. Laws were made to put an end to ambiguity, and that each man might know what he had to expect. How well have they answered this purpose? Let us instance in the article of property. Two men go to law for a certain estate. They would not go to law if they had not both of them an opinion of the success. But we may suppose them partial in their own case. They would not continue to go to law if they were not both promised success by their lawyers. Law was made that a plain man might know what he had to expect; and yet the most skilful practitioners differ about the event of my suit. It will sometimes happen that the most celebrated pleader in the kingdom, or the first counsel in the service of the crown, shall assure me of infallible success, five minutes before another law-officer, styled the keeper of the king's conscience, by some unexpected juggle decides it against me. Would the issue have been equally uncertain if I had had nothing to trust but the plain unperverted sense of a jury of my neighbours, founded in the ideas they entertained of general justice? . . .

A further consideration that will demonstrate the absurdity of law in its most general acceptation is that it is of the nature of prophecy. Its task is to describe what will be the actions of mankind, and to dictate decisions respecting them. . . . The language of such a procedure is 'We are so wise that we can draw no additional knowledge from circumstances as they occur, and we pledge ourselves that, if it be otherwise, the additional knowledge we acquire shall produce no effect upon our conduct'. . . . Law tends, no less than creeds, catechisms and tests, to fix the human mind in a stagnant condition, and to substitute a principle of permanence in the room of that unceasing progress which is the only salubrious element of mind . . . assume to itself the right of distorting or adding to those rules, there law is evidently a less necessary institution. The rules of justice would be more clearly and effectively taught by an actual intercourse with human society, unrestrained by the fetters of prepossession, than they can be by catechisms and codes.

The fable of Procrustes presents us with a faint shadow of the perpetual effort of law. In defiance of the great principle of natural philosophy, that there are not so much as two atoms of matter of the same form through the whole universe, it endeavours to reduce the actions of men, which are composed of a thousand evanescent elements, to one standard. . . . There is no more real justice in endeavouring to reduce the actions of men into classes than there was in the scheme to which we have just alluded, of reducing all men to the same stature. If, on the contrary, justice be a result flowing from the contemplation of all the circumstances of each individual case, if only the criterion of justice be general utility, the inevitable consequence is that the more we have of justice, the more we shall have of truth, virtue and happiness.

From all these considerations we can scarcely hesitate to conclude that law is an institution of the most pernicious tendency.

The subject will receive some additional elucidation if we consider the perniciousness of law in its immediate relation to those who practise it. If there ought to be no such thing as law, the profession of lawyer is no doubt entitled to our disapprobation. A lawyer can scarcely fail to be a dishonest man. This is less a subject for censure than for regret. Men are, in an eminent degree, the creatures of the circumstances under which they are placed. He that is habitually goaded by the incentives of vice will not fail to be vicious. He that is perpetually conversant in quibbles, false colours and sophistry cannot equally cultivate the generous emotions of the soul, and the nice discernment of rectitude. If a single individual can be found who is but superficially tainted with the contagion, how many men on the other hand in whom there appeared a promise of the sublimest virtues have by this trade been rendered indifferent to consistency or accessible to a bribe?[19]

When the philosophy of law shall be properly understood, the true key to its spirit and history will probably be found, not, as some men have

---

19 *P.J.*, Bk. VII, ch. viii.

fondly imagined, in a desire to secure the happiness of mankind, but in the venal compact by which superior tyrants have purchased the countenance and alliance of the inferior.[20]

Can there be a more flagrant injury than to inscribe, as we do in effect, upon our courts of judgment, 'This is the Hall of Justice, in which the principles of right and wrong are daily and systematically slighted, and offences of a thousand different magnitudes are confounded together, by the insolent supineness of the legislator, and the unfeeling selfishness of those who have engrossed the produce of the general labour to their particular emolument!'[21]

Among my melancholy reflections I tasked my memory, and counted over the doors, the locks, the bolts, the chains, the massy walls and grated windows that were between me and liberty. These, said I, are the engines that tyranny sits down in cold and serious meditations to invent. This is the empire that man exercises over man. Thus is a being, formed to expatiate, to act, to smile and enjoy, restricted and benumbed. How great must be his depravity or heedlessness who vindicates this scheme for changing health and gaiety and serenity, into the wanness of a dungeon and the deep furrows of agony and despair!

Thank God, exclaims the Englishman, we have no Bastille! Thank God, with us no man can be punished without a crime! Unthinking wretch! Is that a country of liberty where thousands languish in dungeons and fetters? Go, go, ignorant fool and visit the scenes of our prisons! Witness their unwholesomeness, their filth, the tyranny of their governors, the misery of their inmates! After that show me the man shameless enough to triumph, and say, England has no Bastille![22]

Strange, that men from age to age should consent to hold their lives at the breath of another, merely that each in his turn may have a power of acting the tyrant according to law! Oh, God! Give me poverty! Shower upon me all the imaginary hardships of human life! I will receive them all with thankfulness. Turn me a prey to the wild beasts of the desert, so

---

20 *P.J.*, Bk. VII, ch. v.
21 *P.J*, Bk. VII, ch. iv.
22 *Caleb Williams*, Vol. II, ch. xi.

I be never again the victim of man dressed in the gore-dripping robes of authority! Suffer me at least to call life and the pursuits of life my own! Let me hold it at the mercy of elements, of the hunger of beasts or the revenge of barbarians, but not the cold-blooded prudence of monopolists and kings![23]

7 Punishment

The doctrine of necessity [that man could not have acted otherwise than he has acted] will teach us to look upon punishment with no complacence, and at all times to prefer the most direct means of encountering error, the development of truth. . . .

It is usually imagined that, independently of the supposed utility of punishment, there is proper desert in the criminal, a certain fitness in the nature of things that renders pain the suitable concomitant of vice. It is therefore frequently said that it is not enough that a murderer should be transported to a desert island, where there should be no danger that his malignant propensities should ever again have opportunity to act; but that it is also right the indignation of mankind against him should express itself in the infliction of some actual ignominy and pain. On the contrary, under the system of necessity, the terms, guilt, crime, desert and accountableness, in the abstract and general sense in which they have sometimes been applied, have no place.[24]

Punishment is often used to signify the voluntary infliction of evil upon a vicious being, not merely because the public advantage demands it, but because there is apprehended to be a certain fitness and propriety in the nature of things that render suffering, abstractedly from the benefit to result, the suitable concomitant of vice. The justice of punishment, however, in this import of the word, can only be a deduction from the hypothesis of free will, if indeed that hypothesis will sufficiently support it; and must be false, if human actions are necessary. Mind, as was sufficiently apparent when we treated of that subject, is an agent in no other sense than matter is an agent. It operates and is operated upon, and the nature, the force and line of direction of the first, is exactly in proportion to the nature, force and line of direction of the second.

---

23 *Caleb Williams*, Vol. III, ch. i.
24 *P.J.*, Bk. IV, ch. viii.

Morality, in a rational and designing mind, is not essentially different from morality in an inanimate substance. A man of certain intellectual habits is fitted to be an assassin; a dagger of a certain form is fitted to be his instrument. . . . The assassin cannot help the murder he commits, any more than the dagger.[25]

Punishment for example is liable to all the objections which are urged against punishment for restraint or reformation, and to certain other objections peculiar to itself. It is employed against a person not now in the commission of an offence, and of whom we can only suspect that he ever will offend. It supersedes argument, reason and conviction, and requires us to think such a species of conduct our duty, because such is the good pleasure of our superiors, and because, as we are taught by the example in question, they will make us rue our stubbornness if we think otherwise. In addition to this it is to be remembered that, when I am made to suffer as an example to others, I am myself treated with super-cilious neglect, as if I were totally incapable of feeling and morality.[26]

It is difficult to express the abhorrence [corporal punishment] ought to create. The genuine propensity of man is to venerate mind in his fellow man. With what delight do we contemplate the progress of intellect, its efforts for the discovery of truth, the harvest of virtue that springs up under the genial influence of instruction, the wisdom that is gener-ated through the medium of unrestricted communication? How com-pletely do violence and corporal infliction reverse the scene? From this moment, all the wholesome avenues of mind are closed, and on every side we see them guarded with a train of disgraceful passions, hatred, revenge, despotism, cruelty, hypocrisy, conspiracy and cowardice. Man becomes the enemy of man; and stronger are seized with the lust of unbridled domination, and the weaker shrink, with hopeless disgust, from the approach of a fellow. With what feelings must an enlightened observer contemplate the furrow of a lash imprinted upon the body of a man?[27]

---

25 *P.J.*, Bk. VII, ch. i.
26 *P.J.*, Bk. VII, ch. iii.
27 *P.J.*, Bk. VII, ch. vi.

8 Obedience and Authority

To understand the subject of obedience with sufficient accuracy, it is necessary that we should attend to the various shades of meaning of which the word is susceptible. Every voluntary action is an act of obedience; in performing it, we comply with some view, and are guided by some incitement or motive.

The purest kind of obedience is where an action flows from the independent conviction of our private judgment, where we are directed, not by the precarious and mutable interference of another, but by a recollection of the intrinsic and indefeasible tendency of the action to be performed. In this case the object of obedience is the dictate of the understanding: the action may, or may not, be such as my neighbours of the community will approve, but this approbation does not constitute its direct motive.

The kind of obedience which stands next to this in its degree of voluntariness arises in the following manner. Every man is capable of comparing himself with his fellows. Every man will find that there are some points in which he is the equal or perhaps the superior of other men, but that there are certainly some points in which other men are superior to him. The superiority in question in the present instance is superiority of intellect or information. It may happen that the point in which another man surpasses me is a point of some importance to my welfare or convenience. I want, for example, to build a house, or to sink a well. It may happen that I have not leisure or means to acquire the science necessary for this purpose. Upon that supposition I am not to be blamed if I employ a builder for the first, or a mechanic for the second; nor shall I be liable to blame if I work in person under his direction. This sort of obedience is distinguished by the appellation of confidence; and to justify, in a moral view, the reposing of confidence, the only thing necessary is that it should be fitter and more beneficial, all things considered, that the function to be performed should be performed by another person, than it should be performed by me.

The third and last kind of obedience necessary to be adverted to upon the present occasion is where I do that which is not prescribed to me by my private judgment, merely on account of the mischievous consequences that I foresee will be annexed to my omission by the arbitrary interference of some voluntary being.

The most important observation that arises upon the statement of this scale of obedience is that obedience in the second degree ought to be guarded with as much jealousy, and kept by the person yielding obedience within as narrow limits, as possible. The last sort of obedience will frequently be necessary. . . . Yet obedience flowing from the consideration of a penalty is less a source of degradation and depravity than a habit of obedience founded in confidence. The man who yields to it, may reserve, in its most essential sense, his independence. He may be informed in judgment, and resolved in purpose, as to every moral and social obligation. He may suffer his understanding neither to be seduced nor confounded; he may observe, in its fullest extent, the mistake and prepossession of his neighbour, to which he thus finds it necessary to accommodate himself. It seems possible that he who thus pities the folly, while he complies with the necessity, may still, even under this discipline, grow in discrimination and sagacity.

The greatest mischief that can arise in the progress of obedience is, where shall it lead us, in any degree, to depart from the independence of our understanding, a departure which general and unlimited confidence necessarily includes. In this view, the best advice that could be given to a person in a state of subjection is, 'Comply, where the necessity of the case demands it; but criticise while you comply. Obey the unjust mandates of your governors; for this prudence and a consideration of the common safety may require; but treat them with no false lenity, regard them with no indulgence. Obey; this may be right; but beware of reverence. Reverence nothing but wisdom and skill: government may be vested in the fittest persons; then they are entitled to reverence, because they are wise, and not because they are governors: and it may be vested in the worst. Obedience will occasionally be right in both cases: you may run south, to avoid a wild beast advancing in that direction, though you want to go north. Be upon your guard against confounding things so totally unconnected with each other as a purely political obedience and respect. Government is nothing but regulated force; force is its appropriate claim upon your attention. It is the business of individuals to persuade; the tendency of concentrated strength is only to give consistency and permanence to an influence more compendious than persuasion.'

All this will be made somewhat clearer if we reflect on the proper correlative of obedience, authority; and here let us recur to the three sorts of obedience above specified.

The first kind of authority, then, is the authority of reason, what is really such, or is only conceived to be such. The terms, both authority and obedience, are less frequently employed in this sense than in either of the following.

The second species of authority is that which depends for its validity upon the confidence of him with whom it prevails, and is where, not having myself acquired such information as to enable me to form a judicious opinion, I yield a greater or less degree of deference to the known sentiment and decision of another. This seems to be the strictest and most precise meaning of the word authority; as obedience, in its most refined sense, denotes that compliance which is the offspring of respect.

Authority in the last of the three senses alluded to is where a man, in issuing his precept, does not deliver that which may be neglected with impunity; but his requisition is attended with a sanction, and the violation of it will be followed with a penalty. This is the species of authority which properly connects itself with the idea of government. It is a violation of political justice to confound the authority which depends upon force, with the authority which arises from reverence and esteem; the modification of my conduct which might be due in the case of a wild beast, with the modification which is due to superior wisdom. These kinds of authority may happen to vest in the same person; but they are altogether distinct and independent of each other. . . .

To a government, therefore, that talked to us of deference to political authority, and honour to be rendered to our superiors, our answer should be: 'It is yours to shackle the body, and restrain our external actions; that is a restraint we understand. Announce your penalties; and we will make our election of submission or suffering. But do not seek to enslave our minds. Exhibit your force in its plainest form, for that is your province; but seek not to inveigle and mislead us. Obedience and external submission is all you are entitled to claim; you can have no right to extort our deference, and command us not to see, and disapprove of, your errors.'[28]

9 Freedom of Thought and Expression

Opinion is the castle, or rather the temple, of human nature; and, if it be polluted, there is no longer anything sacred or venerable in sublunary existence. If opinion be rendered a topic of political superintendence, we are immediately involved in a slavery to which no imagination of

---

28 *P.J.*, Bk. III, ch. vi.

man can set a termination. The hopes of our improvement are arrested; for government fixes the mercurialness of man to an assigned station. We can no longer enquire or think; for enquiry and thought are uncertain in their direction, and unshackled in their termination. We sink into motionless inactivity and the basest cowardice; for our thoughts and words are beset on every side with penalty and menace.

Is there anything that can look with a more malignant aspect upon the general welfare than an institution tending to give permanence to certain systems and opinions? Such institutions are two ways pernicious; first, which is most material, because they render the future advances of mind inexpressibly tedious and operose; secondly because, by violently confining the stream of reflection and holding it for a time in an unnatural state, they compel it at last to rush forward with impetuosity, and thus occasion calamities which, were it free from restraint, would be found extremely foreign to its nature. If the interference of positive institution had been out of the question, would the progress of intellect, in past ages, have been so slow as to have struck the majority of ingenious observers with despair? . . .

Truth and virtue are competent to fight their own battles. They do not need to be nursed and patronized by the hand of power. . . . Whoever saw an instance in which error, unallied to power, was victorious over truth? Who is there that can bring himself to believe that, with equal arms, truth can be ultimately defeated?[29]

It is one of the first privileges of an Englishman, one of the first duties of a rational being, to discuss with perfect freedom, all the principles proposed to be enforced upon general observance, when those principles are first disclosed, and before they have, by any solemn and final proceeding, been made part of a regular established system.[30]

There can be no enquiry and no science, if I am to be told at the commencement of my studies, in what inference they must all terminate. Labouring under this restraint, I cannot examine; labouring under this restraint, I cannot, strictly speaking, even attempt to examine. . . .

---

29 *P.J.*, Bk. VI, ch. i.
30 William Godwin, *Cursory Strictures* (London: C. and G. Kearsley, 1794), 3.

What men imagine they see in the way of argument, they can scarcely refrain from speaking, and they ought to be permitted to publish. . . . It is a well known maxim of literature, that no principle upon any controversial subject, can be so securely established, as when its adversaries are permitted to attack it, and it is found superior to every objection. A sober and confidential observer will have strange thoughts that suggest themselves to him, respecting the most venerable and generally received maxims, if he find that every person who ventures to enter upon an impartial examination of them, is threatened with the pillory.[31]

Toleration, and freedom of opinion, are scarcely worth accepting, if, when my neighbour differs from me, I do not indeed burn him, but I take every occasion to insult him. There could be no freedom of opinion, if everyone conducted himself thus. Toleration in its full import, requires, not only that there shall be no laws to restrain opinion, but that forbearance and liberality shall be moulded into the manners of the community.[32]

10 Patriotism

One of the most essential principles of political justice is diametrically the reverse of that which imposters, as well as patriots [like Rousseau], have too frequently agreed to recommend. Their perpetual exhortation has been, 'Love your country. Sink the personal existence of individuals in the existence of the community. Make little account of the particular men of whom the society consists, but aim at the general wealth, prosperity and glory. Purify your mind from the gross ideas of sense, and elevate it to the single contemplation of that abstract individual, of which particular men are so many detached members, valuable only for the place they fill.'

The lessons of reason on this head are different from these. Society is an ideal existence, and not, on its own account, entitled to the smallest regard. The wealth, prosperity and glory of the whole are unintelligible chimeras. Set no value on anything but in proportion as you are convinced of its tendency to make individual men happy and virtuous. Benefit, by every practicable mode, man wherever he exists; but be not

---

31 *Considerations*, 36–38.
32 *The Enquirer*, 340.

deceived by the specious idea of affording services to a body of men, for which no individual man is the better. Society was instituted, not for the sake of glory, not to furnish splendid materials for the page of history, but for the benefit of its members. The love of our country, as the term has usually been understood, has too often been found to be one of those specious illusions which are employed by imposters for the purpose of rendering the multitude the blind instruments of their crooked designs.[33]

With the majority of the human species, a kind of selfish impulse of pride and vain-glory, which assumes the form of patriotism, and represents to our imagination whatever is gained to our country as so much gained to our darling selves, leads to a spirit of hatred and all uncharitableness towards the countries around us. We rejoice in their oppression, and make a jubilee, venting our joy in a hundred forms of extravagance, when the bleeding carcasses of thousands of their miserable natives are strewed upon the plain. This sort of patriotism, in its simplest and most uninstructed exhibition, vents itself in uttering hisses, and perhaps casting stones at the unprotected foreigner as he passes along our streets. I do not regard a patriotism of this kind with much feeling of approbation.[34]

11 Monarchy

All kings have possessed such a portion of luxury and ease, have so far been surrounded with servility and falsehood, and to such a degree exempt from personal responsibility, as to destroy the natural and wholesome complexion of the human mind. Being placed so high, they find but one step between them and the summit of social authority, and they cannot but eagerly desire to pass that step. Having so frequent occasions of seeing their commands implicitly obeyed, being trained in so long a scene of adulation and servility, it is impossible they should not feel some indignation at the honest firmness that sets limits to their omnipotence. But to say, 'that every king is a despot in his heart' will presently be shown to be the same thing as to say, that every king is, by unavoidable necessity, the enemy of the human race.[35]

---

33 *P.J.*, Bk. V, ch. xvi.
34 *Thoughts*, 33.
35 *P.J.*, Bk. V, ch. iii.

Again, if kings were exhibited simply as they are in themselves to the inspection of mankind, the 'salutatory prejudice', as it has been called [by Edmund Burke], which teaches us to venerate them would speedily be extinct: it has therefore been found necessary to surround them with luxury and expense. Thus luxury and expense are made the standard of honour, and of consequence the topics of anxiety and envy. However fatal this sentiment may be to the morality and happiness of mankind, it is one of those illusions which monarchical government is eager to cherish. In reality, the first principle of virtuous feeling, as has been elsewhere said, is the love of independence. He that would be just must, before all things, estimate the objects about him at their true value. But the principle in regal states has been to think your father the wisest of men, because he is your father, and your king the foremost of his species because he is king. The standard of intellectual merit is no longer the man, but his title. To be drawn in a coach of state by eight milk-white horses is the highest of all human claims to our veneration. The same principle inevitably runs through every order of the state, and men desire wealth under a monarchical government for the same reason that, under other circumstances, they would have desired virtue.[36]

12 Aristocracy

Aristocracy, as we have already seen, is intimately connected with an extreme inequality of possessions. No man can be a useful member of society except so far as his talents are employed in a manner conducive to the general advantage. In every society, the produce, the means of contributing to the necessities and conveniences of its members, is of a certain amount. In every society, the bulk at least of its members contribute by their personal exertions to the creation of this produce. What can be more desirable and just than that the produce itself should, with some degree of equality, be shared among them? What more injurious than the accumulating upon a few every means of superfluity and luxury, to the total destruction of the ease, and plain, but plentiful subsistence of the many? It may be calculated that the king, even of a limited monarchy, receives the salary of his office, an income equivalent to the labour of fifty thousand men. Let us set out in our estimate from this point, and figure to ourselves the shares of his counsellors, his

---

36 *P.J.*, Bk. V, ch. vi.

nobles, the wealthy commoners by whom the nobility will be emulated, their kindred and dependents. Is it any wonder that, in such countries, the lower orders of the community are exhausted by the hardships of penury and immoderate fatigue? When we see the wealth of a province spread upon the great man's table, can we be surprised that his neighbours have not bread to satiate the ravings of hunger?

Is this a state of human beings that must be considered as the last improvement of political wisdom? In such a state it is impossible that eminent virtue should not be exceedingly rare. The higher and the lower classes will be alike corrupted by their unnatural situation. But to pass over the higher class for the present, what can be more evident than the tendency of want to contract the intellectual powers? The situation which the wise man would desire, for himself, and for those in whose welfare he was interested, would be a situation of alternate labour and relaxation, labour that should not exhaust the frame, and relaxation that was in no danger of degenerating into indolence. Thus industry and activity would be cherished, the frame preserved in a healthful tone, and the mind accustomed to meditation and improvement. But this would be the situation of the whole human species if the supply of our wants were fairly distributed. Can any system be more worthy of disapprobation than that which converts nineteen-twentieths of them into beasts of burden, annihilates so much thought, renders impossible so much virtue and extirpates so much happiness?

But it may be alleged 'that this argument is foreign to the subject of aristocracy; the inequality of conditions being the inevitable consequence of the institution of property'. It is true that many disadvantages have hitherto flowed out of this institution, in the simplest form in which it has yet existed; but these disadvantages, to whatever they may amount, are greatly aggravated by the operations of aristocracy. Aristocracy turns the stream of property out of its natural course, in following which it would not fail to fructify and gladden, in turn at least, every division of the community; and forwards, with assiduous care, its accumulation in the hands of a very few persons.[37]

---

37 *P.J.*, Bk. V, ch. xiii.

13 Democracy

Democracy is a system of government according to which every member of society is considered as a man, and nothing more. So far as positive regulation is concerned, if indeed that can, with any propriety, be termed regulation, which is the mere recognition of the simplest of all moral principles, every man is regarded as equal. Talents and wealth, wherever they exist, will not fail to obtain a certain degree of influence, without requiring positive institution to second their operation. . . .

Democracy restores to man a consciousness of his value, teaches him, by the removal of authority and oppression, to listen only to the suggestions of reason, gives him confidence to treat all other men with frankness and simplicity, and induces him to regard them no longer as enemies against whom to be upon his guard, but as brethren whom it becomes him to assist. The citizen of a democratical state, when he looks upon the oppression and injustice that prevail in the countries around him, cannot but entertain an inexpressible esteem for the advantages he enjoys, and the most unalterable determination to preserve them. The influence of democracy upon the sentiments of its members is altogether of the negative sort, but its consequences are inestimable.[38]

14 Republicanism

It has been observed that the introduction of a republican government is attended with public enthusiasm and irresistible enterprise. Is it to be believed that equality, the true republicanism, will be less effectual? It is true that in republics this spirit, sooner or later, is found to languish. Republicanism is not a remedy that strikes at the root of the evil. Injustice, oppression and misery can find an abode in those seeming happy seats. But what shall stop the progress of ardour and improvement where the monopoly of property is unknown?[39]

15 Representation

Representation, together with many disadvantages, has this benefit, that it is able, impartially, and with discernment, to call upon the most enlightened part of the nation to deliberate for the whole, and may thus generate a degree of wisdom, and a refined penetration of sentiment,

---

38 *P.J.*, Bk. V, ch. xiv.
39 *P.J.*, Bk. VIII, ch. vi.

which it would have been unreasonable to expect as a result of primary assemblies.[40]

But representative government is necessarily imperfect. It is, as was formerly observed, a point to be regretted, in the abstract notion of civil society, that a majority should overbear a minority, and that the minority, after having opposed and remonstrated, should be obliged practically to submit to that which was the subject of their remonstrance. But this evil, inseparable from political government, is aggravated by representation, which removes the powers of making regulations one step further from the people whose lot it is to obey them. Representation therefore, though a remedy, or rather a palliative, for certain evils, is not a remedy so excellent or complete as should authorise us to rest in it as the highest improvement of which the social order is capable.[41]

16 Ballot

[Secret] ballot is a mode of decision still more censurable than sortition [the act of drawing lots]. It is scarcely possible to conceive a political institution that includes a more direct and explicit patronage of vice. It has been said 'that ballot may in certain cases be necessary to enable a man of a feeble character to act with ease and independence, and to prevent bribery, corrupt influence and faction'. Hypocrisy is an ill remedy to apply to the cure of weakness. A feeble and irresolute character might before be accidental; ballot is a contrivance to render it permanent, and to scatter its seeds over a wider surface. The true remedy for a want of constancy and public spirit is to inspire firmness, not to inspire timidity. Sound and just conceptions, if communicated to the mind with perspicuity, may be expected to be a sufficient basis for virtue. To tell men that it is necessary they should form their decision by ballot is to tell them that it is necessary they should be ashamed of their integrity. If sortition taught us to desert our duty, ballot teaches us to draw a veil of concealment over our performance of it. It points out to us a method of acting unobserved. It incites us to make a mystery of our sentiments. If it did this in the most trivial article, it would not be easy to bring the mischief it would produce, within the limits of calculation. But it

---

40 *P.J.*, Bk. V, ch. xx.
41 *P.J.*, Bk. V, ch. xv.

dictates this conduct in our most important concerns. It calls upon us to discharge our duty to the public with the most virtuous constancy; but at the same time directs us to hide our discharge of it. One of the most beneficial principles in the structure of the material universe will perhaps be found to be its tendency to prevent our withdrawing ourselves from the consequences of our own actions. A political institution that should attempt to counteract this principle would be the only true impiety. How can a man have the love of the public in his heart, without the dictates of that love flowing to his lips? When we direct men to act with secrecy, we direct them to act with frigidity. Virtue will always be an unusual spectacle among men, till they shall have learned to be at all times ready to avow their actions, and assign the reasons upon which they are founded.

If then sortition and ballot be institutions pregnant with vice, it follows that all social decisions should be made by open vote; that, wherever we have a function to discharge, we should reflect on the purpose for which it ought to be exercised; and that, whatever conduct we are persuaded to adopt, especially in affairs of general concern, should, most certainly in matters of routine and established practice, be adopted in the face of the world.[42]

What can be more unreasonable than to demand that argument, the usual quality of which is gradually and imperceptibly to enlighten the mind, should declare its effect in the close of a single conversation [by voting]? No sooner does this circumstance occur than the whole scene changes its character. The orator no longer enquires after permanent conviction, but transitory effect. He seeks rather to take advantage of our prejudices than to enlighten our judgment. That which might otherwise have been a scene of patient and beneficent enquiry is changed into wrangling, tumult and precipitation.

Another circumstance that arises out of the decision by vote is the necessity of constructing a form of words that shall best meet the sentiments, and be adapted to the preconceived ideas, of a multitude of men. What can be conceived at once more ludicrous and disgraceful than the spectacle of a set of rational beings employed for hours together in weighing particles, and adjusting commas? Such is the scene that

---

42 *P.J.*, Bk. VI, ch. x.

is incessantly witnessed in clubs and private societies. In parliaments, this sort of business is usually adjusted before the measure becomes a subject of public inspection. But it does not the less exist; and sometimes it occurs in the other mode, so that, when numerous amendments have been made to suit the corrupt interest of imperious pretenders, the Herculean task remains at last to reduce the chaos into a grammatical and intelligible form.

The whole is then wound up, with that flagrant insult upon all reason and justice, the deciding upon truth by the casting up of numbers. Thus everything that we have been accustomed to esteem most sacred is determined, at best, by the weakest heads in the assembly, but, as it not less frequently happens, through the influence of the most corrupt and dishonourable intentions.[43]

Opulence has two ways of this grosser sort, by which it may enable its possessor to command the man below him—punishment and reward. . . .

The remedy for all this therefore, real or potential, mischief, is said to lie in the vote by ballot, a contrivance, by means of which every man shall be enabled to give his vote in favour of or against any candidate that shall be nominated, in absolute secrecy, without it being possible for anyone to discover on which side the elector decided—nay, a contrivance, by which the elector is invited to practise mystery and concealment, inasmuch as it would seem an impertinence in him to speak out, when the law is expressly constructed to bid him to act and be silent. If he speaks, he is guilty of a sort of libel on his brother-electors, who are hereby implicitly reproached by him for their impenetrableness and cowardice. . . .

I would beg the reader to consider, that the vote by ballot, in its obvious construction, is not a symbol of liberty, but of slavery. What is it, that presents to every eye the image of liberty, and compels every heart to confess: This is the temple where she resides? An open front, a steady and assured look, an habitual and uninterrupted commerce between the heart and the tongue. The free man communicates with his neighbour, not in corners and concealed places, but in market-places and scenes of public resort; and it is thus that the sacred spark is caught from man to man, till all are inspired with a common flame. Communication

---

43 *P.J.*, Bk. V, ch. xxiii.

and publicity are of the essence of liberty; it is the air they breathe; and without it they die.[44]

The institution of ballot is the fruitful parent of ambiguities, equivocations and lies without number.[45]

17 Assemblies

In the first place, the existence of a national assembly introduces the evils of a fictitious unanimity. The public, guided by such an assembly, must act with concert, or the assembly is a nugatory excrescence. But it is impossible that this unanimity can really exist. The individuals who constitute a nation cannot take into consideration a variety of important questions without forming different sentiments respecting them. In reality, all questions that are brought before such an assembly are decided by a majority of votes, and the minority, after having exposed, with all the power of eloquence, and force of reasoning, of which they are capable, the injustice and folly of the measures adopted, are obliged, in a certain sense, to assist in carrying them into execution. Nothing can more directly contribute to the depravation of the human understanding and character. It inevitably renders mankind timid, dissembling and corrupt. He that is not accustomed exclusively to act upon the dictates of his own understanding must fall inexpressively short of that energy and simplicity of which our nature is capable. He that contributes his personal exertions, or his property, to the support of a cause which he believes to be unjust will quickly lose that accurate discrimination, and nice sensibility of moral rectitude, which are the principal ornaments of reason.

Secondly, the existence of national councils produces a certain species of real unanimity, unnatural in its character, and pernicious in its effects. The genuine and wholesome state of mind is to be unloosed from shackles, and to expand every fibre of its frame, according to the independent and individual impressions of truth upon that mind. How great would be the progress of intellectual improvement if men were unfettered by the prejudices of education, unseduced by the influence of a corrupt state of society, and unaccustomed to yield without fear, to the

---

44 *T. M.*, 318–19.
45 *T. M.*, 342.

guidance of truth, however unexplored might be the regions, and unexpected the conclusions to which she conducted us? We cannot advance in the voyage of happiness unless we be wholly at large upon the stream that would carry us thither: the anchor that we first looked upon as the instrument of our safety will, at last, be found to be the means of detaining our progress. Unanimity of a certain sort is the result to which perfect freedom of enquiry is calculated to conduct us; and this unanimity would, in a state of perfect freedom, become hourly more conspicuous. But the unanimity that results from men having a visible standard by which to adjust their sentiments is deceitful and pernicious.

In numerous assemblies, a thousand motives influence our judgments, independently of reason and evidence. Every man looks forward to the effects which the opinions he avows will produce his success. Every man connects himself with some sect or party. The activity of his thought is shackled, at every turn, by the fear that his associates may disclaim him. This effect is strikingly visible in the present state of the British parliament, where men, whose faculties are comprehensive almost beyond all former example, may probably be found influenced by all these motives, sincerely to espouse the grossest and most contemptible errors.

Thirdly, the debates of a national assembly are distorted from their reasonable tenor by the necessity of their being uniformly terminated by a vote. Debate and discussion are, in their own nature, highly conducive to intellectual improvement; but they lose this salutary character, the moment they are subjected to this unfortunate condition. . . .

In the last place, national assemblies will by no means be thought to deserve approbation if we recollect, for a moment, the absurdity of that fiction by which society is considered, as it has been termed, as a moral individual. It is in vain we endeavour to counteract the laws of nature and necessity. A multitude of men, after all our ingenuity, will still remain a multitude of men. Nothing can intellectually unite them, short of equal capacity and identical perception. So long as the varieties of mind shall remain, the force of society can no otherwise be concentrated than by one man, for a shorter or a longer term, taking the lead, of the rest, and employing their force, whether material, or dependent on the weight of their character, in a mechanical manner, just as he would employ the force of a tool or a machine. All government corresponds, in a certain degree, to what the Greeks denominated a tyranny. The difference is that, in despotic countries, mind is depressed by an uniform usurpation;

while, in republics, it preserves a greater portion of its activity, and the usurpation more easily conforms itself to the fluctuations of opinion.[46]

The institution of two houses of assembly is the direct method to divide a nation against itself. One of these houses will, in a greater or less degree, be the asylum of usurpation, monopoly and privilege. Parties would expire, as soon as they were born, in a country where opposition of sentiments, and a struggle of interests, were not allowed to assume the formalities of distinct institution.[47]

18 Political Associations and Parties

In political associations, the object of each man is to identify his creed with that of his neighbour. We learn the Shibboleth of a party. We dare not leave our minds at large in the field of enquiry, lest we should arrive at some tenet disrelished by our party. We have no temptation to enquire. Party has a more powerful tendency than perhaps any other circumstance in human affairs to render the mind quiescent and stationary. Instead of making each man an individual, which the interest of the whole requires, it resolves all understandings into one common mass, and subtracts from each the varieties that could alone distinguish him from a brute machine. Having learned the creed of our party, we have no longer any employment for those faculties which might lead us to detect its errors. We have arrived, in our own opinion, at the last page of the volume of truth; and all that remains is by some means to effect the adoption of our sentiments as the standard of right to the whole of mankind. . . .

There is another circumstance to be mentioned, strongly calculated to confirm this position. A necessary attendant upon political associations is harangue and declamation. A majority of the members of any numerous popular society will look to these harangues as the school in which they are to study, in order to become the reservoirs of practical truth to the rest of mankind. But harangues and declamation lead to passion, and not to knowledge. Truth can scarcely be acquired in crowded halls and amidst noisy debates. Where hope and fear, triumph and resentment, are perpetually afloat, the severer faculties of

46 *P.J.*, Bk. V, ch. xxiii.
47 *P.J.*, Bk. V, ch. xxi.

investigation are compelled to quit the field. Truth dwells with contemplation. We can seldom make much progress in the business of disentangling error and delusion but in sequestered privacy, or in the tranquil interchange of sentiments that takes place between two persons. . . .

It should always be remembered in these cases that all confederate action is of the nature of government, and that consequently every argument of this work, which is calculated to display the evils of government, and to recommend the restraining it within as narrow limits as possible, is equally hostile to political associations. They have also a disadvantage peculiar to themselves, as they are an obvious usurpation upon the rights of the public, without any pretence of delegation from the community at large.[48]

19 Revolutions

Revolution is instigated by a horror against tyranny, yet its own tyranny is not without peculiar aggravations. There is no period more at war with the existence of liberty. The unrestrained communication of opinions has always been subjected to mischievous counteraction, but upon such occasions it is trebly fettered. At other times men are not so much alarmed for its effects. But in a moment of revolution, when everything is in crisis, the influence even of a word is dreaded, and the consequent slavery is complete. Where was there a revolution in which a strong vindication of what it was intended to abolish was permitted, or indeed almost any species of writing or argument, that was not, for the most part, in harmony with the opinions which happened to prevail? An attempt to scrutinize men's thoughts, and punish their opinions, is of all kinds of despotism the most odious; yet this attempt is peculiarly characteristic of a period of revolution.

The advocates of revolution usually remark 'that there is no way to rid ourselves of our oppressors, and prevent new ones from starting up in their room, but by inflicting on them some severe and memorable retribution'. Upon this statement it is particularly to be observed that there will be oppressors as long as there are individuals inclined, either from perverseness, or rooted and obstinate prejudice, to take party with the oppressor. We have therefore to terrify not only the man of crooked ambition but all those who would support him, either from a corrupt

---

48 *P.J.*, Bk. IV, ch. iii.

motive, or a well-intended error. Thus, we propose to make men free; and the method we adopt is to influence them, more rigorously than ever, by the fear of punishment. We say that government has usurped too much, and we organize a government tenfold more encroaching in its principles and terrible in its proceedings. Is slavery the best project that can be devised for making men free? Is a display of terror the readiest mode for rendering them fearless, independent and enterprising? . . .

The duty therefore of the true politician is to postpone revolution if he cannot entirely prevent it. It is reasonable to believe that the later it occurs, and the more generally ideas of political good and evil are previously understood, the shorter, and the less deplorable, will be the mischiefs attendant on revolution. The friend of human happiness will endeavour to prevent violence; but it would be the mark of a weak and valetudinarian temper to turn away our eyes from human affairs in disgust, and refuse to contribute our labours and attention to the general weal, because perhaps, at last, violence may forcibly intrude itself. It is our duty to make a proper advantage of circumstances as they arise, and not to withdraw ourselves because everything is not conducted according to our ideas of propriety. The men who grow angry with corruption, and impatient at injustice, and through these sentiments favour the abettors of revolution, have an obvious apology to palliate their errors; theirs is the excess of a virtuous feeling.[49]

I ought to take up arms against the despot by whom my country is invaded, because my capacity does not enable me by arguments to prevail on him to desist, and because my countrymen will not preserve their intellectual independence in the midst of oppression. For the same reason I ought to take up arms against the domestic spoiler, because I am unable either to persuade him to desist, or the community to adopt a just political institution by means of which security might be maintained consistently with the abolition of punishment.[50]

20 Reform

Oh, Reform! Genial and benignant power! how often has thy name been polluted by profane and unhallowed lips! How often has thy standard

---

49 *P.J.*, Bk. IV, ch. ii.
50 *P.J.*, Bk. VII, ch. v.

been unfurled by demagogues, and by assassins been drenched and disfigured with human gore![51]

The great cause of humanity, which is now pleading in the face of the universe, has but two enemies; those friends of antiquity, and those friends of innovation, who, impatient of suspense, are inclined violently to interrupt the calm, the incessant, the rapid and auspicious progress which thought and reflection appear to be making in the world. Happy would it be for mankind if those persons who interest themselves most zealously in these great questions would confine their exertions to the diffusing, in every possible mode, a spirit of enquiry, and the embracing every opportunity of increasing the stock, and generalizing the communication, of political knowledge![52]

The most sacred of all privileges is that by which each man has a certain sphere, relative to the government of his own actions, and the exercise of his discretion, not liable to be trenched upon by the intemperate zeal or dictatorial temper of his neighbour. To dragoon men into the adoption of what we think right is an intolerable tyranny.[53]

It follows however, from the principles already detailed, that the interests of the human species require a gradual, but uninterrupted change. He who should make these principles the regulators of his conduct would not rashly insist upon the instant abolition of all existing abuses. But he would not nourish them with false praise. He would show no indulgence to their enormities. He would tell all the truth he could discover, in relation to the genuine interests of mankind. Truth, delivered in a spirit of universal kindness, with no narrow resentments or angry invective, can scarcely be dangerous, or fail, so far as relates to its own operation, to communicate a similar spirit to the hearer. Truth, however unreserved be the mode of its enunciation, will be sufficiently gradual in its progress. It will be fully comprehended only by slow degrees by its most assiduous votaries; and the degrees will be still more temperate

---

51 *Considerations*, 18.
52 *P.J.*, Bk. IV, ch. I.
53 *P.J.*, Bk. IV, ch. I.

by which it will pervade so considerable a portion of the community as to render them mature for a change of their own common institutions.[54]

The only method according to which social improvements can be carried on, with sufficient prospect of an auspicious event, is when the improvement of our institutions advances in a just proportion to the illumination of the public understanding. There is a condition of political society best adapted to every different stage of individual improvement. The more nearly this condition is successively realized, the more advantageously will the general interest be consulted. There is a sort of provision in the nature of the human mind for this species of progress. Imperfect institutions, as has already been shown, cannot long support themselves when they are generally disapproved of, and their effects truly understood. There is a period at which they may be expected to decline and expire almost without an effort. Reform, under this meaning of the term, can scarcely be considered as of the nature of action. Men feel their situation; and the restraints that shackled them before vanish like a deception. When such a crisis has arrived, not a sword will need to be drawn, not a finger to be lifted up in purposes of violence. The adversaries will be too few and too feeble to be able to entertain a serious thought of resistance against the universal sense of mankind.[55]

If, in any society, wealth be estimated at its true value, and accumulation and monopoly be regarded as the seals of mischief, injustice and dishonour, instead of being treated as titles to attention and deference, in that society the accommodations of human life will tend to their level, and the inequality of conditions will be destroyed. A revolution of opinions is the only means of attaining to this inestimable benefit. Every attempt to effect this purpose by means of regulation will probably be found ill conceived and abortive. Be this as it will, every attempt to correct the distribution of wealth by individual violence is certainly to be regarded as hostile to the first principles of public security.[56]

---

54 *P.J.*, Bk. III, ch. vii.
55 *P.J.*, Bk. IV, ch. ii.
56 *P.J.*, Bk. VIII, ch. ii.

Persuasion, and not force, is the legitimate instrument for influencing the human mind; and I shall never be justifiable in having recourse to the latter, while there is any rational hope of succeeding by the former.[57]

The inference from this survey of human life is that he who is fully persuaded that pleasure is the only good ought by no means to leave every man to enjoy his peculiar pleasure according to his own peculiar humour. Seeing the great disparity there is between different conditions of human life, he ought constantly to endeavour to raise each class, and every individual of each class, to a class above it. This is the true equalization of mankind. Not to pull down those who are exalted, and reduce all to a naked and savage equality. But to raise those who are abased; to communicate to every man all genuine pleasures, to elevate every man to all true wisdom and to make all men participators of a liberal and comprehensive benevolence. This is the path in which the reformers of mankind ought to travel. This is the prize they should pursue.[58]

The real enemies of liberty in any country are not the people, but those higher orders who find their imaginary profit in a contrary system. Infuse just views of society into a certain number of the liberally educated and reflecting members; give to the people guides and instructors; and the business is done.[59]

Men of genius must rise up, to show their brethren that these evils, though familiar, are not therefore the less dreadful, to analyse the machine of human society, to demonstrate how the parts are connected together, to explain the immense chain of events and consequences, to point out the defects and the remedy. It is thus only that important reforms can be produced. Without talents, despotism would be endless, and public misery incessant. Hence it follows, that he who is a friend to general happiness, will neglect no chance of producing in his pupil or his child, one of the long-looked-for saviours of the human race.[60]

---

57 *P.J.*, Bk. VIII, ch. ii.
58 *P.J.* Bk. IV, ch. xi.
59 *P.J.*, Bk. I, ch. vi.
60 *The Enquirer*, 10–11.

V

ECONOMICS

1 Importance of Property

The subject of property is the key-stone that completes the fabric of political justice. According as our ideas respecting it are crude or correct, they will enlighten us as to the consequences of a *simple form of society without government,* and remove the prejudices that attach us to complexity. There is nothing that more powerfully tends to distort our *judgment* and *opinions* than erroneous notions concerning the goods of fortune. Finally, the period that must put an end to the system of *coercion* and *punishment* is intimately connected with the circumstance of property's being placed upon an equitable basis.[1]

2 Effects of Unequal Distribution

Its first effect is . . . a sense of dependence. It is true that courts are mean-spirited, intriguing and servile, and that this disposition is transferred by contagion from them to all ranks of society. But accumulation brings home a servile and truckling spirit, by no circuitous method, to every house in the nation. Observe the pauper fawning with abject vileness upon his rich benefactor, speechless with sensations of gratitude, for having received that which he ought to have claimed, not indeed with arrogance, or a dictatorial and overbearing temper, but with the spirit of a man discussing with a man, and resting his cause only on the justice of his claim. Observe the servants that follow in a rich man's train, watchful of his looks, anticipating his commands, not daring to reply to his insolence, all their time and their efforts under the direction of his caprice. Observe the tradesman, how he studies the passions of his customers, not to correct, but to pamper them, the vileness of his

---

1   *P.J.*, Bk. VIII ch. i.

flattery and the systematical constancy with which he exaggerates the merit of his commodities. Observe the practices of a popular election, where the great mass are purchased by obsequiousness, by intemperance and bribery, or driven by unmanly threats of poverty and persecution. Indeed 'the age of chivalry' is not 'gone'! The feudal spirit still survives that reduced the great mass of mankind to the rank of slaves and cattle for the service of a few. . . . The ostentation of the rich perpetually goads the spectator to the desire of opulence. Wealth, by the sentiments of servility and dependence it produces, makes the rich man stand forward as the principal object of general esteem and deference. In vain are sobriety, integrity and industry, in vain the sublimest powers of mind, and the most ardent benevolence, if their possessor be narrow in his circumstances. To acquire wealth and to display it is therefore the universal passion. The whole structure of human society is made a system of the narrowest selfishness.[2]

How great are the inequalities that prevail in every country in Europe! How powerful is the incitement held out to the poor man, to commit hostility on the property of the rich, to commit it in detail, each man for himself, or by one great and irresistible effort to reduce every thing to universal chaos![3]

Poverty is an enormous evil. By poverty I understand the state of a man possessing no permanent property, in a country where wealth and luxury have already gained a secure establishment.

He then that is born to poverty, may be said, under another name, to be born a slave.[4]

I need not tell you that I saw no great expressions of cheerfulness in either the elder or younger inhabitants of these walls [of the textile factory]: their occupations were too anxious and monotonous—the poor should not be too much elevated, and incited to forget themselves. There was a kind of stupid and hopeless vacancy in every face: this proceeded from the same causes.

---

2   *P.J.*, Bk. VIII ch. iii.
3   *Considerations*, 4.
4   *The Enquirer*, 162.

Not one of the persons before me exhibited any signs of vigour and robust health. They were all sallow; their muscles flaccid, and their form emaciated. Several of the children appeared to me, judging from their size, to be under four years of age—I never saw such children. . . .

These children were uncouth and ill-grown in every limb, and were stiff and decrepit in their carriage, so as to seem like old men. At four years of age they could earn salt to their bread; but at forty, if it were possible they should live so long, they could not earn bread to their salt. They were made sacrifices, while yet tender; and, like the kid, spoken of by Moses, were seethed and prepared for the destroyer in their mother's milk. This is the case in no state of society, but in manufacturing towns. The children of gipsies and savages have ruddy cheeks and a sturdy form, can run like lapwings, and climb trees with the squirrel.[5]

I saw that in civilized society, the only state that appeared to me worthy of man, he could not subsist but upon the fruits of others' industry or of his own, and that the very attempt to supply himself, subjected him in various ways to the caprice of his fellow-creatures, and was in various ways precarious. I saw that the poor man was strangely pent up and fettered in his exertions, whether their purpose might be to unfold the treasury of intellect in the solitude of his closet, or to collect facts and phenomena by wandering on the face of the earth. I saw that, when he suffered himself to contract the dearer ties of husband and father, poverty and an uncertain subsistence might depress his heart, and corrode his vitals. I saw that, if riches made a man a slave, entire poverty did the same, and perhaps more effectually. It is perhaps within the compass of possibility for a rich man to be free (though almost as hardly, as for 'a camel to pass through the eye of a needle'); but the poor man must always wear the marks of his bolts about him, and drag at every step a heavier and more intolerable chain. I saw that poverty was environed on all sides with temptations, urging and impelling a man, to sell his soul, to sacrifice his integrity to debase the clearness of his spirit, and to become the bond slave of a thousand vices.[6]

---

5 William Godwin, *Fleetwood; or, The New Man of Feeling*, Vol. I (1805), 244–50.
6 *Mandeville*, Vol. I, 256–57.

But, if the rich are seduced and led away from the inspirations of virtue, it may easily be conceived how much more injurious, and beyond the power of control, are the effects on the poor. The mysterious source from which the talents of men are derived, cannot be supposed in their distribution to be regulated by the artificial laws of society, and to have one measure for those which are bestowed upon the opulent, and another for the destitute. . . .

And not only will the germs of excellence be likely to be extinguished in the members of the lower class of the community, but the temptations to irregular acts and incroachments upon the laws for the security of property will often be so great, as to be in a manner irresistible. The man who perceives that, with all his industry, he cannot provide for the bare subsistence of himself and those dependent upon him, while his neighbour revels in boundless profusion, cannot but sometimes feel himself goaded to an attempt to correct this crying evil. What must be expected to become of that general good-will which is the natural inheritance of a well-constituted mind, when urged by so bitter oppression and such unendurable sufferings? The whole temper of the human heart must be spoiled, and the wine of life acquire a quality acrimonious and malignant.

But it is not only in the extreme classes of society that the glaring inequality with which property is shared produces its injurious effects. All those who are born in the intermediate ranks are urged with a distempered ambition, unfavourable to independence of temper, and to true philanthropy. Each man aspires to the improvement of his circumstances, and the mounting, by one step and another, higher in the scale of the community. The contemplations of the mind are turned towards selfishness. In opulent communities we are presented with the genuine theatre for courts and kings. And, wherever there are courts, duplicity, lying, hypocrisy and cringing dwell as in their proper field. Next come trades and professions, with all the ignoble contemplations, the resolved smoothness, servility and falsehood, by which they are enabled to gain a prosperous and triumphant career.[7]

3 Economic Justice

Every man has a right to that, the exclusive possession of which being awarded to him, a greater sum of benefit or pleasure will result than

---

7   *T. M.*, 465–67.

could have arisen from its being otherwise appropriated. . . . If man have a right to anything, he has a right to justice. These terms, as they have ordinarily been used in moral enquiry, are, strictly and properly speaking, convertible terms.

Let us see how this principle will operate in the inferences it authorises us to make. Human beings are partakers of a common nature; what conduces to the benefit or pleasure of one man will conduce to the benefit or pleasure of another. Hence it follows, upon the principles of equal and impartial justice, that the good things of the world are a common stock, upon which one man has as valid a title as another to draw for what he wants. It appears in this respect, as formerly it appeared in the case of our claim to the forbearance of each other, that each man has a sphere the limit and termination of which is marked out by the equal sphere of his neighbour. I have a right to the means of subsistence; he has an equal right. I have a right to every pleasure I can participate without injury to myself or others; his title in this respect is of similar extent.[8]

Suppose, for example, that it is right for one man to possess a greater portion of property than another, whether as the fruit of his industry, or the inheritance of his ancestors. Justice obliges him to regard this property as a trust, and calls upon him maturely to consider in what manner it may be employed for the increase of liberty, knowledge and virtue. He has no right to dispose of a shilling of it at the suggestion of his caprice. So far from being entitled to well-earned applause, for having employed some scanty pittance in the service of philanthropy, he is in the eye of justice a delinquent if he withhold any portion from that service. Could that portion have been better or more worthily employed? That it could is implied in the very terms of the proposition. Then it was just it should have been so employed. . . .

But justice is reciprocal. If it be just that I should confer a benefit, it is just that another man should receive it, and, if I withhold from him that to which he is entitled, he may justly complain. My neighbour is in want of ten pounds that I can spare. There is no law of political institution to reach this case, and transfer the property from me to him. But in a passive sense, unless it can be shown that the money can be

---

8 *P.J.*, Bk. VIII, ch. i.

more beneficently employed, his right is as complete (though actively he have not the same right, or rather duty, to possess himself of it) as if he had my bond in his possession, or had supplied me with goods to the amount.[9]

Every man who invents a new luxury, adds so much to the quality of labour entailed on the lower orders of society. The same may be affirmed of every man who adds a new dish to his table, or who imposes a new tax upon the inhabitants of his country. It is a gross and ridiculous error to suppose that the rich pay for anything. There is no wealth in the world except this, the labour of man. What is misnamed wealth, is merely a power vested in certain individuals by the institutions of society, to compel others to labour for their benefit. So much labour is requisite to produce the necessities of life; so much more to produce those superfluities which at present exist in any country. Every new luxury is a new weight thrown into the scale. The poor are scarcely ever benefited by this. It adds a certain portion to the mass of their labour; but it adds nothing to their conveniences. Their wages are not changed. They are paid no more now for the work of ten hours, than before for the work of eight. They support the burden; but they come in for no share of the fruit.[10]

Money is the representative and the means of exchange to real commodities; it is no real commodity itself. The wages of the labourer and the artisan have always been small; and, as long as the extreme inequality of conditions subsists, will always remain so. If the rich man would substantially relieve the burdens of the poor, exclusive of the improvement he may communicate to their understandings or their temper, it must be by taking upon himself a part of their labour, and not by setting them tasks. All other relief is partial and temporary.[11]

There is no reason to be found in the code of impartial justice, why one man should work, while another man is idle. Mechanical and daily labour is the deadliest foe to all that is great and admirable in the human

9   *P.J.*, Bk. II ch. ii.
10   *The Enquirer*, 177–78.
11   *The Enquirer*, 173.

mind. But the spendthrift is not merely content, that other men should labour, while he is idle . . . he is not satisfied that they should labour for his gratification: he obliges them to do this gratuitously; he trifles with their expectations; he baffles their hopes; he subjects them to a long succession of tormenting uncertainties. They labour indeed; but they do not consume the commodities they produce, nor derive the smallest advantage from their industry. 'We have laboured; and other men have entered into the fruits of our labours.'[12]

The earth is the sufficient means, either by the fruit it produces, or the animals it breeds, of the subsistence of man. A small quantity of human labour, when mixed and incorporated with the bounties of nature, is found perfectly adequate to the purposes of subsistence. This small quantity it is, in the strictness of moral obligation, every man's duty to contribute; unless perhaps, in rare instances, it can be shown that the labour of some, directed to a higher species of usefulness, would be injuriously interrupted by this trivial portion of mechanical and subordinate labour.[13]

The commodities that substantially contribute to the subsistence of the human species, form a very short catalogue. They demand from us but a slender portion of industry. If these only were produced, and sufficiently produced, the species of man would be continued. If the labour necessarily required to produce them were equitably divided among the poor, and still more if it were equitably divided among all, each man's share of labour would be light, and his portion of leisure would be ample. There was a time, when this leisure would have been of small comparative value. It is hoped that the time will come, when it will be applied to the most important purposes. Those hours which are not required for the production of the necessities of life, may be devoted to the cultivation of the understanding, the enlarging our stock of knowledge, the refining our taste, and thus opening to us new and more exquisite sources of enjoyment. It is not necessary that all our hours of leisure should be dedicated to intellectual pursuits; it is probable that the well-being of man would be best promoted by the

---

12 *The Enquirer*, 171.
13 *The Enquirer*, 214.

production of some superfluities and luxuries, though certainly not of such as an ill-imagined and exclusive vanity now teaches us to admire; but there is no reason in the system of the universe or the nature of man, why any individual should be deprived of the means of intellectual cultivation.[14]

4 Degrees of Property

Of property there are three degrees.

The first and simplest degree is that of my permanent right in those things the use of which being attributed to me, a greater sum of benefit or pleasure will result than could have arisen from their being otherwise appropriated. It is of no consequence, in this case, how I came in to possession of them, the only necessary condition being their superior usefulness to me, and that my title to them is such as is generally acquiesced in by the community in which I live. Every man is unjust who conducts himself in such a manner respecting these things as to infringe, in any degree, upon my power of using them, at the time when the using them will be of real importance to me.

It has already appeared that one of the most essential of the rights of man is my right to the forbearance of others; not merely that they shall refrain from everything that may, by direct consequence, affect my life, or the possession of my powers, but that they shall refrain from usurping upon my understanding, and shall leave me a certain equal sphere for the exercise of my private judgment. This is necessary because it is possible for them to be wrong, as well as for me to be so, because the exercise of the understanding is essential to the improvement of man, and because the pain and interruption I suffer are as real, when they infringe, in my conception only, upon what is of importance to me, as if the infringement had been, in the utmost degree, palpable. Hence it follows that no man may, in ordinary cases, make use of my apartment, furniture or garments, or my food, in the way of barter or loan, without having first obtained my consent.

The second degree of property is the empire to which every man is entitled over the produce of his own industry, even that part of it the use of which ought not to be appropriated to himself. It has been repeatedly shown that all the rights of man which are of this description are

---

14 *The Enquirer*, 174–75.

passive. He has no right of option in the disposal of anything which may fall into his hands. Every shilling of his property, and even every, the minutest, exertion of his powers have received their destination from the decrees of justice. He is only the steward.

It will readily be perceived that this second species of property is in a less rigorous sense fundamental than the first.

It is, in one point of view, a sort of usurpation. It vests in me the preservation and dispensing of that which in point of complete and absolute right belongs to you.

The third degree of property is that which occupies the most vigilant attention in the civilized states of Europe. It is a system, in whatever manner established, by which one man enters into the faculty of disposing of the produce of another man's industry. There is scarcely any species of wealth, expenditure or splendour, existing in any civilized country, that is not, in some way, produced by the express manual labour, and the corporeal industry, of the inhabitants of that country. The spontaneous productions of the earth are few, and contribute little to wealth, expenditure or splendour. Every man may calculate, in every glass of wine he drinks, and every ornament he annexes to his person how many individuals have been condemned to slavery and sweat, incessant drudgery, unwholesome food, continual hardships, deplorable ignorance, and brutal insensibility, that he may be supplied with these luxuries. It is a gross imposition that men are accustomed to put upon themselves when they talk of the property bequeathed to them by their ancestors. The property is produced by the daily labour of men who are now in existence. All that their ancestors bequeathed to them was a mouldy patent which they show as a title to extort from their neighbours what the labour of those neighbours has produced.

It is clear therefore that the third species of property is in direct contradiction to the second.

The most desirable state of human society would require that the quantity of manual labour and corporal industry to be exerted, and particularly that part of it which is not the uninfluenced choice of our own judgment, but is imposed upon each individual by the necessity of his affairs, should be reduced within as narrow limits as possible. For any man to enjoy the most trivial accommodation, while, at the same time, a similar accommodation is not accessible to every other member of the community, is, absolutely speaking, wrong. All refinements of luxury, all inventions that tend to give employment to a great number of labouring hands, are directly adverse to the propagation of happiness.[15]

5 Rights of Property

We should recollect the principle in which doctrine of property is founded, the sacred and indefeasible right of private judgment. There are but two objects for which government can rationally be conceived to have been originated first, as a treasury of public wisdom, by which individuals might, in all cases, with advantage be directed, and which might actively lead us, with greater certainty, in the path of happiness: or, secondly, instead of being forward to act itself as an umpire, that the community might fill the humbler office of guardian of the rights of private judgment, and never interpose but when one man appeared, in this respect, alarmingly to encroach upon another. All the arguments of this work have tended to show that the latter, and not the former, is the true end of civil institution. The first idea of property then is a deduction from the right of private judgment; the first object of government is the preservation of this right. Without permitting to every man, to a considerable degree, the exercise of his own discretion, there can be no independence, no improvement, no virtue and no happiness. This is a privilege in the highest degree sacred; for its maintenance, no exertions and sacrifices can be too great. Thus deep is the foundation of the doctrine of property. It is, in the last resort, the palladium of all that ought to be dear to us, and must never be approached but with awe and veneration. He that seeks to loosen the hold of this principle upon our minds, and that would lead us to sanction any exceptions to it with the most deliberate and impartial consideration, however right may be his intentions, is, in that instance, an enemy to the whole.[16]

Property is sacred: there is but one way in which duty requires the possessor to dispose of it, but I may not forcibly interfere, and dispose of it in the best way in his stead. This is the ordinary law of property, as derived from the principles of universal morality. But there are cases that supersede this law. The principle that attributes to every man the disposal of his property, as well as that distributes to every man

---

15 *P.J.*, Bk. VIII, ch. ii.
16 *P.J.*, Bk. VIII, ch. ii.

his sphere of discretion, derives its force in both instances from the consideration that a greater sum of happiness will result from its observance that its infringement. Wherever therefore the contrary to this is clearly the case, there the force of the principle is suspended. What shall prevent me from taking by force from my neighbour's store, if the alternative be that I must otherwise perish with hunger? What shall prevent me from supplying the distress of my neighbour from property that, strictly speaking, is not my own, if the emergence be terrible, and will not admit of delay? Nothing; unless it be the punishment that is reserved for such conduct in some instances; since it is no more fitting that I should bring upon myself calamity and death than that I should suffer them to fall upon another.[17]

6 Population

The question of population, as it relates to the science of politics and society, is considerably curious. Several writers upon these topics have treated it in a way calculated to produce a very gloomy impression, and have placed precautions to counteract the multiplication of the human species among the most important objects of civil prudence.

Perhaps however express precautions . . . are superfluous and nugatory. There is a principle in the nature of human society by means of which everything seems to tend to its level, and to proceed in the most auspicious way, when least interfered with by the mode of regulation. In a certain stage of the social progress, population seems rapidly to increase. . . . In a subsequent stage, it undergoes little change, either in the way of increase or diminution; this is the case in the more civilised countries of Europe. The number of inhabitants in a country will perhaps never be found in the ordinary course of affairs, greatly to increase beyond the facility of subsistence.

Nothing is more easy than to account for this circumstance. So long as there is a facility of subsistence, men will be encouraged to early marriages, and to a careful rearing of their children. . . . In many European countries, on the other hand, a large family has become a proverbial expression for an uncommon degree of poverty and wretchedness. The price of labour in any state, so long as the spirit of accumulation shall prevail, is an infallible barometer of the state of its population.

---

17 *P.J.*, Bk. III, ch. iii.

It is impossible where the price of labour is greatly reduced, and an added population threatens a still further reduction, that men should not be considerably under the influence of fear, respecting an early marriage, and a numerous family.

There are various methods by the practice of which population may be checked; by the exposing of children, as among the ancients . . . by the art of procuring abortion . . . by a promiscuous intercourse of the sexes, which is found extremely hostile to the multiplication of the species; or, lastly, by a systematical abstinence, such as must be supposed, in some degree, to prevail in monasteries of either sex. But, without any express institution of this kind, the encouragement or discouragement that arises from the general state of a community will probably be found to be all-powerful in its operation.

Supposing however that population were not thus adapted to find its own level, it is obvious to remark upon the objection of this chapter that to reason thus is to foresee difficulties at a great distance. Three fourths of the habitable globe are now uncultivated. The improvements to be made in cultivation, and the augmentations the earth is capable of receiving in the article of productiveness, cannot, as yet, be reduced to any limits of calculation. Myriads of centuries of still increasing population may pass away, and the earth be yet found sufficient for the support of its inhabitants. It were idle therefore to conceive discouragement from so distant a contingency.[18]

Let us apply these remarks to the condition of society . . . in which a great degree of equality and an ardent spirit of benevolence are assumed to prevail. We have found that, in the community in which we live, one of the great operative checks upon an increasing population arises from virtue, prudence or pride. Will there be less of virtue, prudence and honourable pride in such a condition of society, than there is at present? It is true, the ill consequences of a numerous family will not come so coarsely home to each man's individual interest, as they do at present. It is true, a man in such a state of society might say, 'if my children cannot subsist at my expense, let them subsist at the expense of my neighbour'. But it is not in the human character to reason after this manner in such a situation. The more men are raised above poverty and a life of

---

18 *P.J.*, Bk. VIII, ch. ix.

expedients, the more decency will prevail in their conduct, and sobriety in their sentiments.

Where everyone has a character, no one will be willing to distinguish himself by headstrong imprudence. Where a man possesses every reasonable means of pleasure and happiness, he will not be in a hurry to destroy his own tranquillity or that of others by thoughtless excess.[19]

If I look to the past history of the world, I do not see that increasing population has produced such convulsions as he [Malthus] predicts from it, or that vice and misery alone have controlled and confined it; and, if I look to the future, I cannot so despair of the virtues of man to submit to the most obvious rules of prudence, or of the faculties of man to strike out remedies as yet unknown, as to convince me that we ought to sit down for ever contented with all oppression, abuses and inequality, which we now find fastened on the necks, and withering the hearts, of so great a portion of our species.[20]

I have endeavoured to show, 1) that we have no authentic documents to prove any increase in the numbers of mankind, and that, if there is any tendency to increase, exclusively of the counteracting causes that are to be traced in the annals of history, which is by no means certain, that tendency is of the most moderate description; 2) that the counteracting causes are neither constant nor regular in their operation, and have nothing in them of an occult and mysterious nature; and, 3) that the means which the earth affords for the subsistence of man, are subject to no assignable limits, and that the nourishment of human beings in civilised society, can never, unless in the case of seasons peculiarly unfavourable, sustain any other difficulty, till the whole globe has been raised to a very high degree of cultivation, except such as arises from political institutions.[21]

---

19 *Thoughts*, 73–74.
20 *Thoughts*, 75–76.
21 *Of Population*, 508.

VI

EDUCATION

1 Power of Education

The state of society is incontestably artificial; the power of one man over another must be always derived from convention, or from conquest; by nature we are equal. The necessary consequence is, that government must always depend upon the opinion of the governed. Let the most oppressed people under heaven once change their mode of thinking, and they are free. But the inequality of parents and children is the law of our nature, eternal and uncontrollable. Government is very limited in its power of making men either virtuous or happy; it is only in the infancy of society that it can do anything considerable; in its maturity it can only direct a few of our outward actions. But our moral dispositions and character depend very much, perhaps entirely, upon education.[1]

It may however reasonably be suspected whether the education of design be not, intrinsically considered, more powerful than the education of accident. If at any time it appear impotent, this is probably owing to mistakes in the project. The instructor continually fails in wisdom of contrivance, or conciliation of manner, or both. It may often happen, either from the pedantry of his habits, or the impatience of his temper, that his recommendation shall operate rather as an antidote than an attraction. Preceptors are apt to pique themselves upon disclosing part and concealing part of the truth, upon a sort of commonplace, cant exhortation to be addressed to youth, which it would be an insult to offer to the understanding of men. But children are not inclined to consider him entirely as their friend whom they detect in an attempt

---

1   *A.S.*, (1783), 2–3.

to impose upon them. Were it not otherwise, were we sufficiently frank and sufficiently skilful, did we apply ourselves to excite the sympathy of the young and to gain their confidence, it is not to be believed but that the systematical measures of the preceptor would have a decisive advantage over the desultory influence of accidental impression. Children are a sort of raw material put into our hands, a ductile and yielding substance, which, if we do not ultimately mould in conformity to our wishes, it is because we throwaway the power committed to us, by the folly with which we are accustomed to exert it. But there is another error not less decisive. The object we choose is an improper one. Our labour is expended, not in teaching truth, but in teaching falsehood. When that is the case, education is necessarily and happily maimed of half its powers. The success of an attempt to mislead can never be complete. We continually communicate in spite of ourselves the materials of just reasoning; reason is the genuine exercise, and truth the native element of an intellectual nature; it is no wonder therefore that, with a crude and abortive plan to govern his efforts, the preceptor is perpetually baffled, and the pupil, who has been thus stored with systematic delusions, and partial, obscure, and disfigured truths, should come out anything rather than that which his instructor intended him.[2]

2 Innocence of Children

The vices of youth spring not from nature, who is equally the kind and blameless mother of all her children; they derive from the defects of education.[3]

No observation is more common, than that mankind are more generous in the earlier periods of their life, and that their affections become gradually contracted the farther they advance in the vale of years. Confidence, kindness, benevolence, constitute the entire temper of youth. And unless these amiable dispositions be blasted in the bud by the baneful institutions of ambition, vanity and pride, there is nothing with which they would not part, to cherish adversity, and remunerate favour.[4]

---

2   *P.J.*, Bk. I, ch. iv.

3   *A.S.*, 52.

4   *A.S.*, 49–50.

Which of you is there, that has not at some time regretted that age, in which a smile is ever upon the countenance, and peace and serenity at the bottom of the heart? How is it you can consent to deprive these little innocents of an enjoyment, that slides so fast away? How is it you can find in your heart to pall these fleeting years with bitterness and slavery.[5]

The undesigning gaiety of youth has the strongest claim upon your humanity. There is not in the world a truer object of pity, than a child terrified at every glance, and watching, with anxious uncertainty, the caprices of a pedagogue. If he survive, the liberty of manhood is dearly bought by so many heartaches. And if he die, happy to escape your cruelty, the only advantage he derives from the sufferings you have inflicted, is that of not regretting a life, of which he knew nothing but torments.

But who is it that has told you, that the certain, or even the probable consequences of this severity are beneficial? Nothing is so easily proved, as that the human mind is pure and spotless, as it came from the hands of God, and that the vices of which you complain, have their real source in those shallow and contemptible precautions, that you pretend to employ against them. Of all the conditions to which we are incident, there is none so unpropitious to whatever is ingenuous and honourable, as that of a slave. It plucks away by the root all sense of dignity, and all manly confidence. In those nations of antiquity, most celebrated for fortitude and heroism, their youth had never their haughty and unsubmitting neck bowed to the inglorious yoke of a pedagogue.[6]

3 Love of Liberty in Children

There is a reverence that we owe to every thing in human shape. I do not say that a child is the image of God. But I do affirm that he is an individual being, with powers of reasoning, with sensations of pleasure and pain, and with principles of morality; and that in this description is contained abundant cause for the exercise of reverence and forbearance. By the system of nature he is placed by himself; he has a claim upon his

5   *A S.*, 23–24.
6   *A.S.*, 24–25.

little sphere of empire and discretion; and he is entitled to his appropriate portion of independence.[7]

But of all the sources of unhappiness to a young person the greatest is a sense of slavery. How grievous the insult, or how contemptible the ignorance, that tells a child that youth is the true season of felicity, when he feels himself checked, controlled, and tyrannised over in a thousand ways? I am rebuked, and my heart is ready to burst with indignation. A consciousness of the power assumed over me, and of the unsparing manner in which it is used, is intolerable. There is no moment free from the danger of harsh and dictatorial interruption; the periods, when my thoughtless heart began to lose the sense of its dependence, seem of all others most exposed to it. There is no equality, no reasoning, between me and my task-master. If I attempt it, it is considered as mutiny. If it be seemingly conceded, it is only the more cutting mockery. He is always in the right; right and power in these trials are found to be inseparable companions. I despise myself for having forgotten my misery, and suffered my heart to be deluded into a transitory joy. Dearly indeed, by twenty years of bondage, do I purchase the scanty portion of liberty, which the government of my country happens to concede to its adult subjects!

The condition of a negro-slave in the West Indies, is in many respects preferable to that of the youthful son of a free-born European. The slave is purchased upon a view of mercantile speculation; and, when he has finished his daily portion of labour, his master concerns himself no further about him. But the watchful care of the parent is endless. The youth is never free from the danger of grating interference.[8]

Liberty is the school of understanding. This is not enough adverted to. Every boy learns more in his hours of play, than in his hours of labour. In school he lays in the materials of thinking; but in his sports he actually thinks: he whets his faculties, and he opens his eyes. The child from the moment of his birth is an experimental philosopher: he essays his organs and his limbs, and learns the use of his muscles. Everyone who will attentively observe him, will find that this is his perpetual

---

7   *The Enquirer*, 88–89.
8   *The Enquirer*, 66–67.

employment. But the whole process depends upon liberty. Put him into a mill, and his understanding will improve no more than that of the horse which turns it. . . . I know that the earth is the great Bridewel of the universe, where spirits, descended from heaven, are committed to drudgery and hard labour. Yet I should be glad that our children, up to a certain age, were exempt; sufficient is the hardship and subjection of their whole future life; methinks, even Egyptian taskmasters would consent that they should grow up in peace, till they had acquired the strength necessary for substantial service.

Liberty is the parent of strength. Nature teaches the child, by the play of the muscles, and pushing out his limbs in every direction, to give them scope to develop themselves. Hence it is that he is so fond of sports and tricks in the open air, and that these sports and tricks are so beneficial to him. He runs, he vaults, he climbs, he practises exactness of eye, and sureness of aim. His limbs grow straight and taper, and his joints well-knit and flexible. The mind of a child is no less vagrant than his steps; it pursues the gossamer, and flies from object to object, lawless and unconfined: and it is equally necessary to the development of his frame, that his thoughts and his body should be free from fetters.[9]

There is another way in which the schoolboy exercises his powers during his periods of leisure. He is often in society; but he is ever and anon in solitude. At no period of human life are our reveries so free and untrammelled, as at the period here spoken of. He climbs the mountain-cliff, and penetrates into the depths of the woods. His joints are well-strung; he is a stranger to fatigue. He rushes down the precipice, and mounts again with ease, as though he had the wings of a bird. He ruminates, and pursues his own trains of reflection and discovery, 'exhausting worlds', as it appears to him, 'and then imagining new'. He hovers on the brink of the deepest philosophy, enquiring how came I here, and to what end. He becomes a castle-builder, constructing imaginary colleges and states, and searching out the businesses in which they are to be employed, and the schemes by which they are to be regulated. He thinks what he would do, if he possessed uncontrollable strength, if he could fly, if he could make himself invisible. In this train of mind he cons his first lessons of liberty and independence. He learns self-reverence, and says to himself,

---

9 *Fleetwood*, 247–49.

I also am an artist, and a maker. He ruffles himself under the yoke, and feels that he suffers foul tyranny when he is driven, and when brute force is exercised upon him, to compel him to a certain course, or to chastise his faults, imputed or real.[10]

4 Nature of Education

Modern education not only corrupts the heart of our youth, by the rigid slavery to which it condemns them, it also undermines their reason, by the unintelligible jargon with which they are overwhelmed in the first instance, and the little attention, that is given to the accommodating their pursuits to their capacities in the second.[11]

All education is despotism. It is perhaps impossible for the young to be conducted without introducing in many cases the tyranny of implicit obedience. Go there; do that; read; write; rise; lie down; will perhaps for ever be the language addressed to youth by age.[12]

5 Evils of National Education

The injuries that result from a system of national education are in the first place, that all public establishments include in them the idea of permanence. They endeavour, it may be, to secure and to diffuse whatever of advantageous to society is already known. If they realized the most substantial benefits at the time of their introduction, they must inevitably become less and less useful as they increased in duration. But to describe them as useless is a very feeble expression of their demerits. They actively restrain the flights of mind, and fix it in the belief of exploded errors. It has frequently been observed of universities, and extensive establishments for the purpose of education, that the knowledge taught there is a century behind the knowledge which exists among the unshackled and unprejudiced members of the same political community. But public education has always expended its energies in the support of prejudice; it teaches its pupils, not the fortitude that shall bring every proposition to the test of examination, but the art of vindicating such tenets as may chance to be established. . . . This feature

---

10 *T. M.*, 190.
11 *A.S.*, 31.
12 *The Enquirer*, 60.

runs through every species of public establishment; and, even in the petty institution of Sunday schools, the chief lessons that are taught are a superstitious veneration for the church of England, and to bow to every man in a handsome coat. All this is directly contrary to the true interests of mankind. All this must be unlearned before we can begin to be wise. . . .

Secondly, the idea of national education is founded in an inattention to the nature of mind. Whatever each man does for himself is done well; whatever his neighbours or his country undertake to do for him is done ill. It is our wisdom to incite men to act for themselves, not to retain them in a state of perpetual pupillage. He that learns because he desires to learn will listen to the instructions he receives, and apprehend their meaning. He that teaches because he desires to teach will discharge his occupation with enthusiasm and energy. But the moment political institution undertakes to assign to every man his place the functions of all will be discharged with supineness and indifference. . . . This whole proposition of national education is founded upon a supposition which has been repeatedly refuted in this work, but which has recurred upon us in a thousand forms, that unpatronised truth is inadequate to the purpose of enlightening mankind.

Thirdly, the project of a national education ought uniformly to be discouraged on account of its obvious alliance with national government. This is an alliance of a more formidable nature than the old and much contested alliance of church and state. Before we put so powerful a machine under the direction of so ambiguous an agent, it behoves us to consider well what it is that we do. Government will not fail to employ it, to strengthen its hands, and perpetuate its institutions. If we could even suppose the agents of government not to propose to themselves an object which will be apt to appear in their eyes, not merely innocent, but meritorious: the evil would not the less happen. Their views as institutors of a system of education will not fail to be analogous to their views in their political capacity: the data upon which their conduct as statesmen is vindicated will be the data upon which their instructions are founded. It is not true that our youth ought to be instructed to venerate the constitution, however excellent; they should be led to venerate truth; and the constitution only so far as it corresponds with their uninfluenced deductions of truth. Had the scheme of a national education been adopted when despotism was most triumphant, it is not to be believed that it could have for ever stifled the voice of truth. But it would have been the most formidable and profound contrivance for that purpose that imagination can suggest. Still, in the countries where liberty chiefly prevails, it is reasonably to be assumed that there are important errors, and a national education has the most direct tendency to perpetuate those errors, and to form all minds upon one model.[13]

6 Teachers

Nothing can be more pitiable than the condition of the instructor in the present modes of education. He is the worst of slaves. He is consigned to the severest of imprisonments. He is condemned to be perpetually engaged in handling and rehandling the foundations of science. Like the unfortunate wretch upon whom the lot has fallen in a city reduced to extremities, he is destroyed that others may live. Among all the hardships he is compelled to suffer, he endeavours to console himself with the recollection that his office is useful and patriotic. But even this consolation is a slender one. He is regarded as a tyrant by those under his jurisdiction, and he is a tyrant. He mars their pleasures. He appoints to each his portion of loathed labour. He watches their irregularities and their errors. He is accustomed to speak to them in tones of dictation and censure. He is the beadle to chastise their follies. He lives alone in the midst of a multitude. His manners, even when he goes into the world, are spoiled with the precision of pedantry and the insolence of despotism. His usefulness and his patriotism therefore, have some resemblance to those of a chimney-sweeper and a scavenger, who, if their existence is of any benefit to mankind, are however rather tolerated in the world, than thought entitled to the testimonies of our gratitude and esteem.[14]

It is the most difficult thing in the world for the schoolmaster to inspire into his pupil the desire to do his best. An overwhelming majority of lads at school are in their secret hearts rebels to the discipline under which they are placed. The instructor draws one way, and the pupil another. The object of the latter is to find out how he may escape censure and punishment with the smallest expense of scholastic application. He looks at the task that is set him, without the most distant

---

13 *P.J.*, Bk. VI, ch. viii.
14 *The Enquirer*, 84–85.

desire of improvement, but with alienated and averted eye. And, where this is the case, the wonder is not that he does not make a brilliant figure. It is rather an evidence of the slavish and subservient spirit incident to the majority of human beings, that he learns any thing. Certainly the schoolmaster, who judges of the powers of his pupil's mind by the progress he makes in what he would most gladly be excused from learning, must be expected perpetually to fall into the most egregious mistakes.[15]

7 Schools

Let me be permitted in this place to observe, that the association of a small number of pupils seems the most perfect mode of education [in existing circumstances]. There is surely something unsuitable to the present state of mankind, in the wishing to educate our youth in perfect solitude. Society calls forth a thousand powers both of mind and body, that must otherwise rust in inactivity. And nothing is more clear from experience, than that there is a certain tendency to moral depravation in very large bodies of this kind, to which there has not yet been discovered a sufficient remedy.[16]

The pupil of private education is commonly either awkward and silent, or pert, presumptuous and pedantical. In either case he is out of his element, embarrassed with himself, and chiefly anxious about how he shall appear. On the contrary, the pupil of public education usually knows himself, and rests upon his proper centre. He is easy and frank, neither eager to show himself, nor afraid of being observed. His spirits are gay and uniform. His imagination is playful, and his limbs are active. Not engrossed by a continual attention to himself, his generosity is ever ready to break out; he is eager to fly to the assistance of others, and intrepid and bold in the face of danger. He has been used to contend only upon a footing of equality; or to endure suffering with equanimity and courage. His spirit therefore is unbroken; while the man, who has been privately educated, too often continues for the remainder of his life timid, incapable of a ready self-possession, and ever prone to prognosticate ill of the contentions in which he may unavoidably be engaged.[17]

---

15 *T.M.*, 34–35.
16 *A.S.*, 52–54.
17 *The Enquirer*, 62–63.

The objections to both the modes of education here discussed are of great magnitude. It is unavoidable to enquire, whether a middle way might no be selected, neither entirely public, nor entirely private, avoiding the mischiefs of each, and embracing the advantages of both. This however is perhaps a subordinate question, and of an importance purely temporary. We have here considered only the modes of education at this time in practice. Perhaps an adventurous and undaunted philosophy would lead to the rejecting them altogether, and pursuing the investigation of a mode totally dissimilar. There is nothing so fascinating in either, as should in reason check the further excursions of our understanding.[18]

8 Method of Teaching

Speak the language of truth and reason to your child, and be under no apprehension for the result. Show him that what you recommend is valuable and desirable, and fear not but he will desire it. Convince his understanding, and you enlist all his powers animal and intellectual in your service. How long has the genius of education been disheartened and unnerved by the pretence that man is born all that it is possible for him to become? How long has the jargon imposed upon the world which would persuade us that in instructing a man you could not add to, but unfold his stores? The miscarriages of education do not proceed from the boundedness of its powers, but from the mistakes with which it is accompanied. We often inspire disgust, where we mean to infuse desire. We are wrapped up in ourselves, and do not observe, as we ought, step by step the sensations that pass in the mind of our hearer. We mistake compulsion for persuasion, and delude ourselves into the belief that despotism is the road to the heart.[19]

Education will proceed with a firm step and with genuine lustre when those who conduct it shall know what a vast field it embraces; when they shall be aware that the effect, the question whether the pupil shall be a man of perseverance and enterprise or a stupid and inanimate dolt, depends upon the powers of those under whose direction he is placed and the skill with which those powers shall be applied.[20]

---

18 *The Enquirer*, 64.
19 *The Enquirer*, 1–3.
20 *P.J.*, Bk. I, ch. iv.

When a child is born, one of the earliest purposes of his institutor ought to be, to awaken his mind, to breathe a soul into the, as yet, unformed mass. . . . If education cannot do everything, it can do much. To the attainment of any accomplishment what is principally necessary, is that the accomplishment should be ardently desired. How many instances is it reasonable to suppose there are, where this ardent fire exists, and the means of attainment are clearly and skilfully pointed out, where yet the accomplishment remains finally unattained? Give but sufficient motive, and you give everything. Whether the object be to shoot at a mark, or to master a science, this observation is equally applicable.

The means of exciting desire are obvious. Has the proposed object desirable qualities? Exhibit them. Delineate them with perspicuity, and delineate them with ardour. Show your object from time to time under every point of view which is calculated to demonstrate its loveliness. Criticise, commend, exemplify.[21]

It seems probable that early instruction is a thing, in itself considered, of very inferior value. Many of those things which we learn in our youth, it is necessary, if we would well understand, that we should learn over again in our riper years. Many things that, in the dark and unapprehensive period of youth, are attained with infinite labour, may, by a ripe and judicious understanding, be acquired with an effort inexpressibly inferior. He who should affirm, that the true object of juvenile education was to teach no one thing in particular, but to provide against the age of five and twenty a mind as well regulated, active, and prepared to learn, would certainly not obtrude upon us the absurdest of paradoxes.

The purpose therefore of early instruction is not absolute. It is of less importance, generally speaking, that a child should acquire this or that species of knowledge, than that, through the medium of instruction, he should acquire habits of intellectual activity. It is not so much for the direct consideration of what he learns, that his mind must not be suffered to lie idle. The preceptor in this respect is like the incloser of uncultivated land; his first crops are not valued for their intrinsic excellence; they are sown that the land might be brought into order. The springs of the mind, like the joints of the body, are apt to grow stiff for want of employment. They must be exercised in various directions and with

---

21 *The Enquirer*, 3–4.

unabating perseverance. In a word, the first lesson of a judicious education is, Learn to think, to discriminate, to remember and to enquire.[22]

The road that a sound understanding would point out to us, as leading
most directly to the confidence of another, is, that we should make
ourselves as much as possible his equals, that our affection towards him
should display itself in the most unambiguous colours, that we should
discover a genuine sympathy in his joys and his sorrows, that we should
not play the part of the harsh monitor and austere censor, that we
should assume no artificial manners, that we should talk in no solemn,
prolix and unfeeling jargon, that our words should be spontaneous, our
actions simple, and our countenance the mirror to our hearts.[23]

9 Learning through Desire

Liberty is one of the most desirable of all sublunary advantages. I would
willingly therefore communicate knowledge, without infringing, or with
as little as possible violence to, the volition and individual judgment of
the person to be instructed.

Again; I desire to excite a given individual to the acquisition of
knowledge. The only possible method in which I can excite a sensitive
being to the performance of a voluntary action, is by the exhibition of
motive.

Motives are of two sorts, intrinsic and extrinsic. Intrinsic motives
are those which arise from the inherent nature of the thing recommended. Extrinsic motives are those which have no constant and unalterable connection with the thing recommended, but are combined with
it by accident or at the pleasure of some individual.

Thus, I may recommend some species of knowledge by a display
of the advantages which will necessarily attend upon its acquisition, or
flow from its possession. Or, on the other hand, I may recommend it
despotically, by allurements or menaces, by showing that the pursuit of
it will be attended with my approbation, and that the neglect of it will
be regarded by me with displeasure.

The first of these classes of motives is unquestionably the best. To
be governed by such motives is the pure and genuine condition of a

---

22 *The Enquirer*, 4–5.
23 *The Enquirer*, 125.

rational being. By exercise it strengthens the judgment. It elevates us with a sense of independence. It causes a man to stand alone, and is the only method by which he can be rendered truly an individual, the creature, not of implicit faith, but of his own understanding.

If a thing be really good, it can be shown to be such. If you cannot demonstrate its excellence, it may well be suspected that you are no proper judge of it. Why should not I be admitted to decide, upon that which is to be acquired by the application of my labour?

Is it necessary that a child should learn a thing, before it can have any idea of its value? It is probable that there is no one thing that it is of eminent importance for a child to learn. The true object of juvenile education, is to provide, against the age of five and twenty, a mind well regulated, active, and prepared to learn. Whatever will inspire habits of industry and observation, will sufficiently answer this purpose. Is it not possible to find something that will fulfil these conditions, the benefit of which a child shall understand, and the acquisition of which he may be taught to define? Study with desire is real activity: without desire it is but the semblance and mockery of activity. Let us not, in the eagerness of our haste to educate, forget all the ends of education.

The most desirable mode of education therefore, in all instances where it shall be found sufficiently practicable, is that which is careful that all acquisitions of the pupil shall be preceded and accompanied by desire. The best motive to learn, is perception of the value of the thing learned. The worst motive, without deciding whether or not it be necessary to have recourse to it, may well be affirmed to be constraint and fear. There is a motive between these, less pure than the first, but not so displeasing as the last, which is desire, not springing from the intrinsic excellence of the object, but from the accidental attractions which the teacher may have annexed to it. . . .

Nothing can be more happily adapted to remove the difficulties of instruction, than that the pupil should first be excited to desire knowledge, and next that his difficulties should be solved for him, and his path cleared, as often and as soon as he thinks proper to desire it.

This plan is calculated entirely to change the face of education. The whole formidable apparatus which has hitherto attended it, is swept away. Strictly speaking, no such characters are left upon the scene as either preceptor or pupil. The boy, like the man, studies because he desires it. He proceeds upon a plan of his own invention, or which, by adopting, he has made his own. Everything bespeaks independence and equality. The man, as well as the boy, would be glad in cases of difficulty to consult a person more informed than himself. That the boy is accustomed almost always to consult the man, and not the man the boy, is to be regarded rather as an accident, than any thing essential. Much even of this would be removed, if we remembered that the most inferior judge may often, by the varieties of his apprehension, give valuable information to the most enlightened. The boy however should be consulted by the man unaffectedly, not according to any preconcerted scheme, or for the purpose of persuading him that he is what he is not.

There are three considerable advantages which would attend upon this species of education.

First, liberty. Three fourths of the slavery and restraint that are now imposed upon young persons would be annihilated at a stroke.

Secondly, the judgment would be strengthened by continual exercise. Boys would no longer learn their lessons after the manner of parrots. No one would learn without a reason, satisfactory to himself: why he learned; and it would perhaps be well, if he were frequently prompted to assign his reasons. Boys would then consider for themselves, whether they understood what they read. To know when and how to ask a question is no contemptible part of learning. Sometimes they would pass over difficulties, and neglect essential preliminaries; but then the nature of the thing would speedily recall them, and induce them to return to examine the tracts which before had been overlooked. For this purpose it would be well that the subjects of their juvenile studies should often be discussed, and that one boy should compare his progress and his competence to decide in certain points with those of another. There is nothing that more strongly excites our enquiries than this mode of detecting our ignorance.

Thirdly, to study for ourselves is the true method of acquiring habits of activity. The horse that goes round in a mill, and the boy that is anticipated and led by the hand in all his acquirements, are not active. I do not call a wheel that turns round fifty times a minute, active. Activity is a mental quality. If therefore you would generate habits of activity, turn the boy loose in the fields of science. Let him explore the path for himself. Without increasing his difficulties, you may venture to leave him for a moment, and suffer him to ask himself the question before he asks you, or, in other words, to ask the question before he receives the information. Far be it from the system here laid down, to increase the difficulties of youth. No, it diminishes them a hundred fold. Its office is to produce inclination; and a willing temper makes every burden light. Lastly, it is the tendency of this system to produce in the young, when they are grown up to the stature of men, a love of literature. The established modes of education produce the opposite effect, unless in a fortunate few, who, by the celerity of their progress, and the distinctions they obtain, perhaps escape from the general influence. But, in the majority of cases, the memory of our slavery becomes associated with the studies we pursued, and it is not till after repeated struggles, that those things can be rendered the objects of our choice, which were for so long a time the themes of compulsion.[24]

10 Education in a Free Society

Let us consider the way in which this state of society will modify education. It may be imagined that the abolition of the present system of marriage would make education, in a certain sense, the affair of the public; though, if there be any truth in the reasonings of this work, to provide for it by the positive institutions of a community would be extremely inconsistent with the true principles of an intellectual nature. Education may be regarded as consisting of various branches. First, the personal cares which the helpless state of an infant requires. These will probably devolve upon the mother; unless, by frequent parturition, or by the nature of these cares, that be found to render her share of the burden unequal; and then it will be amicably and willingly participated by others. Secondly, food and other necessary supplies. These will easily find their true level, and spontaneously flow, from the quarter that is deficient. Lastly, the term education may be used to signify instruction. The task of instruction, under such a form of society, will be greatly simplified and altered from what it is at present. It will then scarcely be thought more necessary to make boys slaves than to make men so. The business will not then be to bring forward so many adepts in the egg-shell, that the vanity of parents may be flattered by hearing their praises. No man will think of vexing with premature learning the feeble and inexperienced, lest, when they came to years of discretion, they should refuse to be learned. The mind will be suffered to expand itself

24 *The Enquirer*, 76–81.

in proportion as occasion and impression shall excite it, and not tortured and enervated by being cast in a particular mould. No creature in human form will be expected to learn anything but because he desires it, and has some conception of its value; and every man, in proportion to his capacity, will be ready to furnish such general hints and comprehensive views as will suffice for the guidance and encouragement of him who studies from the impulse of desire.[25]

---

25 *P.J.*, Bk. VIII, ch. viii.

VII

FREE SOCIETY

1 Freedom

An objection that has often been urged against a system of equality is 'that it is inconsistent with personal independence. Every man, according to his scheme, is a passive instrument in the hands of the community. He must eat and drink, and play and sleep, at the bidding of others. He has no habitation, no period at which he can retreat into himself, and not ask another's leave. He has nothing that he can call his own, not even his time or his person. Under the appearance of a perfect freedom from oppression and tyranny, he is in reality subjected to the most unlimited slavery'.

To understand the force of this objection it is necessary that we should distinguish two sorts of independence, one of which may be denominated natural, and the other moral. Natural independence, a freedom from all constraint, except that of reasons and inducements presented to the understanding, is of the utmost importance to the welfare and improvement of mind. Moral independence, on the contrary, is always injurious. The dependence, which is essential, in this respect, to the wholesome temperament of society, includes in it articles that are, no doubt, unpalatable to a multitude of the present race of mankind, but that owe their unpopularity only to weakness and vice. It includes a censure to be exercised by every individual over the actions of another, a promptness to enquire into and judge them. Why should we shrink from this? What could be more beneficial than for each man to derive assistance for correcting and moulding his conduct from the perspicacity of his neighbours? The reason that this species is at present exercised with illiberality is because it is exercised clandestinely, and because we submit to its operation with impatience and aversion. Moral independence is always injurious: for, as has abundantly appeared in the course of the present enquiry, there is no situation in which I can be placed where it is not incumbent upon me to adopt a certain conduct in preference to all others, and, of consequence, where I shall not prove an ill member of society if I act in any other than a particular manner. The attachment that is felt by the present race of mankind to independence in this respect, and the desire to act as they please, without being accountable to the principles of reason, are highly detrimental to the general welfare.

But, if we ought never to act independently of the principles of reason, and, in no instance, to shrink from the candid examination of another, it is nevertheless essential that we should, at all times, be free to cultivate the individuality, and follow the dictates, of our own judgment. If there be anything in the idea of equality that infringes this principle, the objection ought probably to be conclusive. If the scheme be, as it has often been represented, a scheme of government, constraint and regulation, it is, no doubt, in direct hostility with the principles of this work.[1]

Superficial thinkers lay great stress upon the external situation of men, and little upon their internal sentiments. Persevering enquiry will probably lead to a mode of thinking the reverse of this. To be free is a circumstance of little value, if we could suppose men in a state of external freedom, without the magnanimity, energy and firmness that constitute almost all that is valuable in a state of freedom. On the other hand, if a man have these qualities, there is little left for him to desire. He cannot be degraded; he cannot readily become either useless or unhappy. He smiles at the impotence of despotism; he fills up his existence with serene enjoyment and industrious benevolence. Civil liberty is chiefly desirable as a means to procure and perpetuate this temper of mind. They therefore begin at the wrong end, who make haste to overturn and confound the usurped powers of the world. Make men wise, and by that very operation you make them free. Civil liberty follows as a consequence of this; no usurped power can stand against the artillery of opinion. Everything then is in order, and succeeds at its appointed time. How unfortunate is it that men are so eager to strike and have so little constancy to reason![2]

---

1   *P.J.*, Bk. VIII, ch. vii.
2   *P.J.*, Bk. IV, ch. i.

Independence is the best birthright of man, and that which each of us ought to cherish beyond all earthly possessions.

I will tell you what a slave is, and what is a free man. A slave is he who watches with abject spirit the eye of another: he waits timidly, till another man shall have told him, whether he is to be happy or miserable today: his comforts and his peace depend on the breath of another's mouth. No man can be this slave unless he pleases. If by the caprice of fortune he has fallen as to externals into another's power, still there is a point that at his own will he can reserve. He may refuse to crouch; he may walk fearless and erect; the words that he utters may be supplied by that reason, to which the high and low, the rich and the poor, have equally access. And, if he that the misjudging world calls a slave, may retain all that is most substantial in independence, is it possible, that he whom circumstances have made free, should voluntarily put the fetters on his own feet, the manacles on his own hands, and drink the bitter draught of subjection and passive obedience?[3]

2 Anarchy

It is incumbent upon us to remark that anarchy as it is usually understood [in the sense of violent disorder], and a well conceived form of society without government, are exceedingly different from each other. If the government of Great Britain were dissolved tomorrow, unless that dissolution were the result of consistent and digested views of political justice previously disseminated among the inhabitants, it would be very far from leading to the abolition of violence. . . .

Anarchy in its own nature is an evil of short duration. The more horrible are the mischiefs it inflicts, the more does it hasten to a close. But it is nevertheless necessary that we should consider both what is the quality of mischief it produces in a given period, and what is the scene in which it promises to close. The first victim that is sacrificed at its shrine is personal security. Every man who has a secret foe ought to dread the dagger of the foe. There is no doubt that in the worst anarchy multitudes of men will sleep in happy obscurity. But woe to him who by whatever means excites the envy, the jealousy or the suspicion of his neighbour! Unbridled ferocity instantly marks him for its prey. This is indeed the principal evil of such a state, that the wisest, the brightest,

3   *Mandeville*, 148–49.

the most generous and bold will often be most exposed to an immature fate. In such a state we must bid farewell to the patient lucubrations of the philosopher, and the labour of the midnight oil. All is here, like the society in which it exists, impatient and headlong. Mind will frequently burst forth, but its appearance will be like the coruscations of the meteor, not like the mild and equable illumination of the sun. Men, who start forth into sudden energy, will resemble the state that brought them to this unlooked for greatness. They will be rigorous, unfeeling and fierce; and their ungoverned passions will often not stop at equality, but incite them to grasp at power.

With all these evils, we must not hastily conclude, that the mischiefs of anarchy are worse than those which government is qualified to produce. With respect to personal security anarchy is certainly not worse than despotism, with this difference that despotism is as perennial as anarchy is transitory. . . .

There is one point remaining in which anarchy and despotism are strongly contrasted with each other. Anarchy awakens thought, and diffuses energy and enterprise through the community, though it does not effect this in the best manner, as its fruits, forced into ripeness, must not be expected to have the vigorous stamina of true excellence. . . .

One of the most interesting questions in relation to anarchy is that of the manner in which it may be expected to terminate. The possibilities as to this termination are as wide as the various schemes of society which the human imagination can conceive. Anarchy may and has terminated in despotism; and in that case the introduction of anarchy will only serve to afflict us with variety of evils. It may lead to a modification of despotism, a milder and more equitable government than that which has gone before. And it does not seem impossible that it should lead to the best form of human society, that the most penetrating philosopher is able to conceive. Nay, it has something in it that suggests the likeness, a distorted and tremendous likeness, of true liberty. Anarchy has commonly been generated by the hatred of oppression. It is accompanied with a spirit of independence. It disengages men from prejudice and implicit faith, and in a certain degree incites them to an impartial scrutiny into the reason of their actions.[4]

---

4   *P.J.* (1793) Bk. VII, ch. v.

Society for the greater part carries on its own organization. Each man pursues his proper occupation, and there are few individuals that feel the propensity to interrupt the pursuits of their neighbours by personal violence. When we observe the quiet manner in which the inhabitants of a great city, and, in the country, the frequenters of the fields, the high roads, and the heaths, pass along, each engrossed by his private contemplations, feeling no disposition to molest the strangers he encounters, but on the contrary prepared to afford them every courteous assistance, we cannot in equity do less than admire the innocence of our species, and fancy that, like the patriarchs of old, we have fallen in with 'angels unawares'.

There are a few men in every community, that are sons of riot and plunder, and for the sake of these the satirical and censorious throw a general slur and aspersion upon the whole species.

When we look at human society with kind and complacent survey, we are more than half tempted to imagine that men might subsist very well in clusters and congregated bodies without the coercion of law; and in truth criminal laws were only made to prevent the ill-disposed few from interrupting the regular and inoffensive proceedings of the vast majority.[5]

3 Decentralization

The appearance which mankind, in a future state of improvement, may be expected to assume is a policy that, in different countries, will wear a similar form, because we have all the same faculties and the same wants, but a policy the independent branches of which will extend their authority over a small territory, because neighbours are best informed of each others concerns, and are perfectly equal to their adjustment. No recommendation can be imagined of an extensive rather than a limited territory, except that of external security.

Whatever evils are included in the abstract idea of government, they are all of them extremely aggravated by the extensiveness of its jurisdiction, and softened under circumstances of an opposite nature. Ambition, which may be no less formidable than a pestilence in the former, has no room to unfold itself in the latter. Popular commotion is like the waters of the earth, capable where the surface is large, of

---

5 *T. M.*, 112–13.

producing the most tragical effects, but mild and innocuous when confined within the circuit of a humble lake. Sobriety and equity are the
obvious characteristics of a limited role.

It may indeed be objected 'that great talents are the offspring of
great passions, and that, in the quiet mediocrity of a petty republic, the
powers of intellect may be expected to subside into inactivity'. This
objection, if true, would be entitled to the most serious consideration.
But it is to be considered that, upon the hypothesis here advanced, the
whole human species would constitute, in some sense, one great republic, and the prospects of him who desired to act beneficially upon a great
surface of mind would become more animating than ever.[6]

In reality, provided the country were divided into convenient districts
with a power of sending representatives to the general assembly, it
does not appear that any ill consequences would ensue to the common
cause from these districts being permitted to regulate their internal
affairs, in conformity to their own apprehensions of justice. Thus, that
which was at first, a great empire with legislative unity would speedily
be transformed into a confederacy of lesser republics, with a general
congress or Amphictyonic council, answering the purpose of a point
of co-operation upon extraordinary occasions. The ideas of a great
empire, and legislative unity, are plainly the barbarous remains of the
days of military heroism. In proportion as political power is brought
home to the citizens, and simplified into something of the nature of
parish regulation, the danger of misunderstanding and rivalship will
be nearly annihilated. In proportion as the science of government
is divested of its present mysterious appearances, social truth will
become obvious, and the districts pliant and flexible to the dictates of
reason. . . .

A great assembly, collected from the different provinces of an
extensive territory, and constituted the sole legislator of those by whom
the territory is inhabited, immediately conjures up to itself an idea of
the vast multitude of laws that are necessary for regulating the concerns
of those whom it represents. A large city, impelled by the principles of
commercial jealousy, is not slow to digest the volume of its by-laws and
exclusive privileges. But the inhabitants of a small parish, living with

---

6   *P.J.*, Bk. V, ch. xxii.

some degree of that simplicity which best corresponds to the real nature and wants of a human being, would soon be led to suspect that general laws were unnecessary, and would adjudge the causes that came before them, not according to certain axioms previously written, but according to the circumstances and demand of each particular cause.[7]

If communities, instead of aspiring, as they have hitherto done, to embrace vast territory, and glut their vanity with ideas of empire, were contented with a small district, with a proviso of confederation in cases of necessity, every individual would then live under the public eye; and the disapprobation of his neighbours, a species of coercion not derived from the caprice of men but from the system of the universe, would inevitably oblige him either to reform or to emigrate.[8]

4 Administration of Justice and Defence

Government can have no more than two legitimate purposes, the suppression of injustice against individuals within the community, and the common defence against external invasion. The first of these purposes, which alone can have an uninterrupted claim upon us, is sufficiently answered by an association, of such an extent, as to afford room for the institution of a jury to decide upon the offences of individuals within the community, and upon the questions and controversies respecting property which may chance to arise. It might be easy indeed for an offender to escape from the limits of so petty a jurisdiction; and it might seem necessary, at first, that the neighbouring parishes,* or jurisdictions, should be governed in a similar manner, or at least should be willing, whatever was their form of government, to co-operate with us in the removal or reformation of an offender whose present habits were alike injurious to us and to them. But there will be no need of any express compact, and still less of any common centre of authority, for this purpose. General justice, and mutual interest, are found more capable of binding men than signatures and seals. In the

---

7   *P.J.*, Bk. VI, ch. vii.

8   *P.J.*, Bk. VII, ch. iii.

*   The word parish is here used without regard to its origin, and merely in consideration of its being a word descriptive of a certain small portion of territory, whether in population or extent, which custom has rendered familiar to us.

meantime, all necessity for causing the punishment of the crime, to pursue the criminal would soon, at least, cease, if it ever existed. The motives to offence would become rare: its aggravations few: and rigour superfluous.

The principal object of punishment is restraint upon a dangerous member of the community; and the end of this restraint would be answered by the general inspection that is exercised by the members of a limited circle over the conduct of each other, and by the gravity and good sense that would characterize the censures of men, from whom all mystery and empiricism were banished. No individual would be hardy enough in the cause of vice to defy the general consent of sober judgment that would surround him. It would carry despair to his mind, or, which is better, it would carry conviction. He would be obliged, by a force not less irresistible than whips and chains, to reform his conduct.

In this sketch is contained the rude outline of political government. Controversies between parish and parish would be, in an eminent degree, unreasonable, since, if any question arose, about limits, for example, the obvious principles of convenience could scarcely fail to teach us to what district any portion of land should belong. No association of men, so long as they adhered to the principles of reason, could possibly have an interest in extending their territory. If we would produce attachment in our associates, we can adopt no surer method than that of practising the dictates of equity and moderation; and, if this failed in any instance, it could only fail with him who, to whatever society he belonged, would prove an unworthy member. The duty of any society to punish offenders is not dependent upon the hypothetical consent of the offender to be punished, but upon the duty of necessary defence.

But however irrational might be the controversy of parish with parish in such a state of society, it would not be the less possible. For such extraordinary emergencies therefore, provision ought to be made. These emergencies are similar in their nature to those of foreign invasion. They can only be provided against by the concert of several districts declaring and, if needful, enforcing the dictates of justice.

One of the most obvious remarks that suggests itself, upon these two cases, of hostility between district and district, and of foreign invasion which the interest of all calls upon them jointly to repel, is that it is their nature to be only of occasional recurrence, and that therefore the provisions to be made respecting them need not be, in the strictest sense, of perpetual operation.[9]

National assemblies, or, in other words, assemblies instituted for the joint purpose of adjusting the differences between district and district, and of consulting respecting the best mode of repelling foreign invasion, however necessary to be had recourse to upon certain occasions, ought to be employed as sparingly as the nature of the case will admit. They should either never be elected but upon extraordinary emergencies, like the dictator of the ancient Romans, or else sit periodically, one day for example in a year, with a power of continuing their sessions within a certain limit, to hear the complaints and representations of their constituents. The former of these modes is greatly preferred.[10]

5 Dissolution of Government

It remains for us to consider what is the degree of authority necessary to be vested in such a modified species of national assembly as we have admitted into our system. Are they to issue their commands to the different members of the confederacy? Or is it sufficient that they should invite them to co-operate for the common advantage, and, by arguments and addresses, convince them of the reasonableness of the measures they propose? The former of these might at first be necessary. The latter would afterwards become sufficient. The Amphictyonic council of Greece possessed no authority but that which flowed from its personal character. In proportion as the spirit of party was extirpated, as the restlessness of public commotion subsided, and as the political machine became simple, the voice of reason would be secure to be heard. An appeal, by the assembly, to the several districts, would not fail to unite the approbation of reasonable men unless it contained in it something so evidently questionable as to make it perhaps desirable that it should prove abortive.

This remark leads us one step further. Why should not the same distinctions between commands and invitations, which we have just made in the case of national assemblies, be applied to the particular assemblies or juries of the several districts? At first, we will suppose

---

9   *P.J.*, Bk. V, ch. xxii.
10 *P.J.*, Bk. V, ch. xxiii.

that some degree of authority and violence would be necessary. But this necessity does not appear to arise out of the nature of man, but out of the institutions by which he has been corrupted. Man is not originally vicious. He would not refuse to listen to, or be convinced by, the expostulations that are addressed to him, had he not been accustomed to regard them as hypocritical, and to conceive that, while his neighbour, his parent and his political governor pretended to be actuated by a pure regard to his interest or pleasure, they were, in reality, at the expense of his, promoting their own. Such are the fatal effects of mysteriousness and complexity. Simplify the social system in the manner which every motive but those of usurpation and ambition powerfully recommends; render the plain dictates of justice level to every capacity remove the necessity of implicit faith; and we may expect the whole species to become reasonable and virtuous. It might then be sufficient for juries to recommend a certain mode of adjusting controversies, without assuming the prerogative of dictating that adjustment. It might then be sufficient for them to invite offenders to forsake their errors. If their expostulations proved, in a few instances, ineffectual, the evils arising out of this circumstance would be of less importance than those which proceed from the perpetual violation of the exercise of private judgment. But, in reality, no evils would arise: for, where the empire of reason was so universally acknowledged, the offender would either readily yield to the expostulations of authority; or, if he resisted, though suffering no personal molestation, he would feel so uneasy, under the unequivocal disapprobation, and observant eye, of public judgment, as willingly to remove to a society more congenial to his errors.

The reader has probably anticipated the ultimate conclusion from these remarks. If juries might at length cease to decide, and, be contented to invite, if force might gradually be withdrawn and reason trusted alone, shall we not one day find that juries themselves and every other species of public institution may be laid aside as unnecessary? Will not the reasonings of one wise man be as effectual as those of twelve? Will not the competence of one individual to instruct his neighbours be a matter of sufficient notoriety, without the formality of an election? Will there be many vices to correct, and much obstinacy to conquer? This is one of the most memorable stages of human improvement. With what delight must every well informed friend of mankind look forward to the auspicious period, the dissolution of political government, of that brute engine which has been the only perennial cause of the vices of mankind, and which, as has abundantly appeared in the progress of the present work, has mischiefs of various sorts incorporated with its substance, and no otherwise removable than by its utter annihilation![11]

6 Social Arrangements

If superfluity were banished, the necessity for the greater part of the manual industry of mankind would be superseded; and the rest, being amicably shared among the active and vigorous members of the community, would be burdensome to none. Every man would have a frugal, yet wholesome diet; every man would go forth to that moderate exercise of his corporal functions that would give hilarity to the spirits; none would be made torpid with fatigue, but all would have leisure to cultivate the kindly and philanthropical affections, and to let loose his faculties in the search of intellectual improvement.[12]

This argument will be strengthened if we reflect on the amount of labour that a state of equality will require. What is this quantity of exertion from which the objection supposes many individuals to shrink? It is so light as rather to assume the guise of agreeable relaxation and gentle exercise than of labour. In such a community, scarcely anyone can be expected, in consequence of his situation or avocations, to consider himself as exempted from the obligation to manual industry. There will be no rich man to recline in indolence, and fatten upon the labour of his fellows. The mathematician, the poet and the philosopher will derive a new stock of cheerfulness and energy from the recurring labour that makes them feel they are men. There will be no persons devoted to the manufacture of trinkets and luxuries; and none whose office it should be to keep in motion the complicated machine of government.[13]

The object, in the present state of society, is to multiply labour; in another state, it will be to simplify it. . . .

From the sketch which has been given, it seems by no means impossible that the labour of every twentieth man in the community would be

---

11   *P.J.*, Bk. V, ch. xxiv.
12   *P.J.*, Bk. VIII, ch. ii.
13   *P.J.*, Bk. VIII, ch. vi.

sufficient to supply to the rest all the absolute necessaries of life. If then this labour, instead of being performed by so small a number, were amicably divided among the whole, it would occupy the twentieth part of every man's time. Let us compute that the industry of a labouring man engrosses ten hours in every day, which, when we have deducted his hours of rest, recreation and meals, seems an ample allowance. It follows that half an hour a day employed in manual labour by every member of the community would sufficiently supply the whole with necessaries. Who is there that would shrink from this degree of industry? Who is there that sees the incessant industry exerted in this city and island, and would believe that, with half an hour's industry *per diem,* the sum of happiness to the community at large might be much greater than at present? Is it possible to contemplate this fair and generous picture of independence and virtue, where every man would have ample leisure for the noblest energies of mind, without feeling our very souls refreshed with admiration and hope?[14]

Leisure will be multiplied; and the leisure of a cultivated understanding is the precise period in which great designs, designs the tendency of which is to secure applause and esteem, are conceived. In tranquil leisure, it is impossible for any but the sublimest mind to exist without the passion for distinction. This passion, no longer permitted to lose itself in indirect channels and useless wanderings, will seek the noblest course, and perpetually fructify the seeds of public good. Mind, though it will perhaps at no time arrive at the termination of its possible discoveries and improvements, will nevertheless advance with a rapidity and firmness of progression of which we are, at present, unable to conceive the idea.[15]

Everything that is usually understood by the term co-operation is, in some degree, an evil. A man in solitude is obliged to sacrifice or postpone the execution of his best thoughts, in compliance with his necessities, or his frailties. How many admirable designs have perished in the conception, by means of this circumstance? It is still worse when a man is also obliged to consult the convenience of others. If I be expected to

---

14   *P.J.*, Bk. VIII, ch. vi.
15   *P.J.*, Bk. VIII, ch. vi.

eat or to work in conjunction with my neighbour, it must either be at a time most convenient to me, or to him, or to neither of us. We cannot be reduced to a clockwork uniformity.

Hence it follows that all supererogatory co-operation is carefully to be avoided, common labour and common meals. 'But what shall we say to a co-operation that seems dictated by the nature of the work to be performed?' It ought to be diminished. There is probably considerably more of injury in the concert of industry than of sympathies. At present, it is unreasonable to doubt that the consideration of the evil of co-operation is, in certain urgent cases, to be postponed to that urgency. Whether, by the nature of things, co-operation of some sort will always be necessary is a question we are scarcely competent to decide. At present, to pull down a tree, to cut a canal, to navigate a vessel, require the labour of many. Will they always require the labour of many? When we recollect the complicated machines of human contrivance, various sorts of mills, of weaving engines, steam engines, are we not astonished at the compendium of labour they produce? Who shall say where this species of improvement must stop? At present, such inventions alarm the labouring part of the community; and they may be productive of temporary distress, though they conduce, in the sequel, to the most important interests of the multitude. But, in a state of equal labour, their utility will be liable to no dispute. Hereafter it is by no means clear that the most extensive operations will not be within the reach of one man; or to make use of a familiar instance, that a plough may not be turned into a field, and perform its office without the need of superintendence. It was in this sense that the celebrated [Benjamin] Franklin conjectured that 'mind would one day become omnipotent over matter'.[16]

The truth is that a system of equality requires no restrictions or super-intendence. There is no need of common labour, meals or magazines. These are feeble and mistaken instruments for restraining the conduct without making conquest of the judgment. If you cannot bring over the hearts of the community to your party, expect no success from brute regulations. If you can, regulation is unnecessary. Such a system was well enough adapted to the military constitution of Sparta; but it is wholly unworthy of men enlisted in no cause but that of reason and

---

16 *P.J.*, Bk. VIII, ch. viii Appendix.

justice. Beware of reducing men to the state of machines. Govern them through no medium but that of inclination and conviction.[17]

The love of liberty obviously leads to a sentiment of union, and a disposition to sympathize in the concerns of others. The general diffusion of truth will be productive of general improvement; and men will daily approximate towards those views according to which every object will be appreciated at its true value. Add to which, that the improvement of which we speak is public, and not individual. The progress is the progress of all. Each man will find his sentiments of justice and rectitude echoed by the sentiments of his neighbours.[18]

It is accumulation that forms men into one common mass, and makes them fit to be played upon like a brute machine. Were this stumbling-block removed, each man would be united to his neighbour, in love, and mutual kindness, a thousand times more than now: but each man would think and judge for himself.[19]

In a state of society where men lived in the midst of plenty, and where all shared alike the bounties of nature . . . the narrow principle of selfishness would vanish. No man being obliged to guard his little store, or provide, with anxiety and pain, for his restless wants, each would lose his individual existence, in the thought of the general good. No man would be an enemy to his neighbour, for they would have no subject of contention; and of consequence, philanthropy would resume the empire which reason assigns her. Mind would be delivered from perpetual anxiety about corporal support, and free to expatiate in the field of thought which is congenial to her. Each would assist the enquiries of all.[20]

The men therefore whom we are supposing to exist, when the earth shall refuse itself to a more extended population, will probably cease to propagate. The whole will be a people of men, and not of children.

---

17 *P.J.*, Bk. VIII, ch. viii.
18 *P.J.*, Bk. VIII, ch. x.
19 *P.J.*, Bk. VIII, ch. iii.
20 *P.J.*, Bk. VIII, ch. iii.

Generation will not succeed generation, nor truth have, in a certain degree, to recommence her career every thirty years. Other improvements may be expected to keep pace with those of health and longevity. There will be no war, no crimes, no administration of justice, as it is called, and no government. Beside this, there will be neither disease, anguish, melancholy, nor resentment. Every man will seek, with ineffable ardour, the good of all. Mind will be active and eager, yet never disappointed. Men will see the progressive advancement of virtue and good, and feel that, if things occasionally happen contrary to their hopes, the miscarriage itself was a necessary part of that progress. They will know that they are members of the chain, that each has his several utility, and they will not feel indifferent to that utility. They will be eager to enquire into the good that already exists, the means by which it was produced, and the greater good that is yet in store. They will never want motives for exertion; for that benefit which a man thoroughly understands and earnestly loves he cannot refrain from endeavouring to promote.[21]

---

21 *P.J.*, Bk. VIII, ch. ix.

FURTHER READING

Much of the vast amount of commentary on William Godwin is uneven, and I only mention here the works I consider to be the best. The most penetrating essay on Godwin is by William Hazlitt in *The Spirit of the Age* (1825). C. Kegan Paul's *William Godwin: His Friends and Contemporaries* (1876) is an invaluable source book, especially for its letters, but offers little analysis. H.N. Brailsford's *Shelley, Godwin and their Circle* (1931) is a fine introduction, short and sympathetic. George Woodcock's *William Godwin: A Biographical Study* (1946) brings out well Godwin's importance as an anarchist thinker but relies heavily on secondary sources. David Fleischer's able *William Godwin: A Study in Liberalism* (1951) has been superseded by John P. Clark's *The Philosophical Anarchism of William Godwin* (1977), which provides an excellent critical exposition of Godwin's moral and political theory. Don Locke's *A Fantasy of Reason: The Life and Thought of William Godwin* (1980) rightly stresses the value of Godwin's ethics but absurdly claims that he is dead as a political theorist.

William St Clair's *The Godwins and the Shelleys* (1989) is a worthwhile biography of the families, largely based on family archives. My own *William Godwin: Philosopher, Novelist, Revolutionary* (1984, 2017) attempts a comprehensive account of Godwin's life and work and argues that he is the most profound exponent of philosophical anarchism.

Of recent editions of Godwin's *Enquiry concerning Political Justice,* F.E.L. Priestley's introduction (Toronto, 1946) is good on Godwin's philosophy; K. Codell Carter's (Oxford, 1971) and Mark Philp's (Oxford, 2013) are perceptive on Godwin's ethics; but Isaac Kramnick's (Harmondsworth, 1976) is misleading on Godwin's anarchism.

Reflecting the renewed interest in Godwin, there are the *Collected Novels and Memoirs of William Godwin,* in eight volumes, edited by Mark

Philp and others (1992), as well as the *Political and Philosophical Writings of William Godwin*, in seven volumes, also edited by Mark Philp and others (1993). Pamela Clemit has edited *The Letters of William Godwin, Vol. 1: 1778–1797* (Oxford, 2011) and *The Letters of William Godwin, Vol. 2: 1798–1805* (Oxford, 2014). Four more volumes of Godwin's letters are planned. PM Press are also publishing a new edition with corrections of my study, *William Godwin: Philosopher, Novelist, Revolutionary*.

The diary of Godwin, which he kept from 1788 to 1836, has been edited by Victoria Myers, David O'Shaughnessy and Mark Philp and is now available on the website of the Bodleian Library, Oxford (2010). See http//godwindiary.bodleian.ox.ac.uk.

BIBLIOGRAPHY OF WILLIAM
GODWIN'S PRINCIPAL WORKS

In the following list I give the works which I think will be of greatest interest and value today. Place of publication London, unless otherwise stated.

An account of the Seminary that will be opened on Monday the Fourth Day of August, at Epsom in Surrey (1783). Reprinted in *Four Early Pamphlets* (1783–84), edited by B.R. Pollin (Gainesville, 1966).

An Enquiry concerning Political Justice, and its influence on General Virtue and Happiness (2 vols., 1793).

Enquiry concerning Political Justice, and its Influence on Morals and Happiness (2nd ed., 2 vols., 1796; 3rd ed., 2 vols., 1798) The third edition was reprinted with an introduction by F.E.L. Priestley (3 vols., Toronto, 1946); abridged and edited by K. Codell Carter (Oxford, 1971); edited by Isaac Kramnick (Harmondsworth, 1976). Woodstock reprinted a facsimile of the first 1793 edition in two volumes (Oxford and New York, 1992). Mark Philp edited the first 1793 edition (Oxford, 2013) after writing a useful study of *Godwin's Political Justice* (1986).

Things as They Are; or, The Adventures of Caleb Williams (3 vols., 1794). Reprinted as *Caleb Williams*, edited by David McCracken (Oxford, 1970); Maurice Hindle (1998); Pamela Clemit (Oxford, 2009).

Cursory Strictures on Lord Chief Justice Eyre's Charge to the Grand Jury (1794). Reprinted in *Uncollected Writings* (1785–1822), edited by J.W. Marken & B.R. Pollin (Gainesville, 1968).

Considerations on Lord Grenville's and Mr Pitt's Bills concerning Treasonable and Seditious Practices, and Unlawful Assemblies, by a Lover of Order (1794). Reprinted in *Uncollected Writings*, op. cit.

The Enquirer. Reflections on Education, Manners and Literature. In a Series of Essays (1797; 2nd ed., 1823). Reprinted (New York, 1965).

Memoirs of the Author of a Vindication of the Rights of Woman (1798; 2nd ed. 1798). Reprinted with introduction by W. Clark Durrant (1927); paperback (2015).

St. Leon: A Tale of the Sixteenth Century (4 vols., 1799; 4th ed., 1831).

Thoughts Occasioned by the Perusal of Dr Parr's Spital Sermon . . . being a Reply to the Attacks of Dr Parr, Mr Mackintosh, the Author of an Essay on Population, and Others (1801). Reprinted in *Uncollected Writings, op. cit.*

Life of Geoffrey Chaucer (2 vols., 1803; 2nd ed., 4 vols., 1804).

Fleetwood; or, The New Man of Feeling (3 vols., 1805; 2nd ed., 1832).

Mandeville: A Tale of the Seventeenth Century in England (3 vols., Edinburgh, 1817).

Of Population: An Enquiry concerning the Power of Increase in the Numbers of Mankind, being an Answer to Mr Malthus's Essay on that Subject (1820).

History of the Commonwealth of England. From its Commencement, to the Restoration of Charles the Second (4 vols., 1824–28).

Thoughts on Man, his Nature, Productions and Discoveries (1831). Reprinted (New York, 1969).

Four Early Pamphlets (1783–84), edited by B.R. Pollin (Gainesville, 1966).

Uncollected Writings (1785–1822), edited by J.W. Marken & B.R. Pollin (Gainesville, 1968).

Collected Novels and Memoirs of William Godwin, 8 vols., edited by Mark Philp and others (1992).

Political and Philosophical Writings of William Godwin, 7 vols., edited by Mark Philp and others (1993).

ABOUT THE AUTHOR

Peter Marshall is a historian, philosopher, travel writer and poet. He has written sixteen books which have been translated into as many different languages. *Demanding the Impossible: A History of Anarchism* and *William Godwin: Philosopher, Novelist, Revolutionary* have both been republished by PM Press. His other works include *Nature's Web: Rethinking our Place on Earth*, *Riding the Wind: Liberation Ecology for a New Era* and *William Blake: Visionary Anarchist*.

His circumnavigation of Africa was made into a British television series, and an Italian series was based on his work on alchemy, *The Philosopher's Stone*. His latest book is *Poseidon's Realm: A Voyage around the Aegean*. He was a founder member of a libertarian community in England. He has a doctorate in the history of ideas and has taught part-time philosophy and literature at several British universities. His website is www.petermarshall.net.

John P. Clark is an eco-communitarian anarchist theorist and activist. He is the author or editor of fourteen books, including *Anarchy, Geography, Modernity: Selected Writings of Elisée Reclus* (PM Press) and most recently *The Tragedy of Common Sense* (Changing Suns Press).

INDEX

'Passim' (literally 'scattered') indicates intermittent discussion of a topic over a cluster of pages.

ABOUT PM PRESS

PM Press was founded at the end of 2007 by a small collection of folks with decades of publishing, media, and organizing experience. PM Press co-conspirators have published and distributed hundreds of books, pamphlets, CDs, and DVDs. Members of PM have founded enduring book fairs, spearheaded victorious tenant organizing campaigns, and worked closely with bookstores, academic conferences, and even rock bands to deliver political and challenging ideas to all walks of life. We're old enough to know what we're doing and young enough to know what's at stake.

We seek to create radical and stimulating fiction and non-fiction books, pamphlets, T-shirts, visual and audio materials to entertain, educate, and inspire you. We aim to distribute these through every available channel with every available technology—whether that means you are seeing anarchist classics at our bookfair stalls, reading our latest vegan cookbook at the café, downloading geeky fiction e-books, or digging new music and timely videos from our website.

PM Press is always on the lookout for talented and skilled volunteers, artists, activists, and writers to work with. If you have a great idea for a project or can contribute in some way, please get in touch.

PM Press, PO Box 23912, Oakland, CA 94623, www.pmpress.org

FRIENDS OF PM PRESS

These are indisputably momentous times—the financial system is melting down globally and the Empire is stumbling. Now more than ever there is a vital need for radical ideas.

Friends of PM allows you to directly help impact, amplify, and revitalize the discourse and actions of radical writers, filmmakers, and artists. It provides us with a stable foundation from which we can build upon our early successes and provides a much-needed subsidy for the materials that can't necessarily pay their own way. You can help make that happen—and receive every new title automatically delivered to your door once a month—by joining as a Friend of PM Press. And, we'll throw in a free T-shirt when you sign up.

Here are your options:

- **$30 a month** Get all books and pamphlets plus 50% discount on all webstore purchases

- **$40 a month** Get all PM Press releases (including CDs and DVDs) plus 50% discount on all webstore purchases

- **$100 a month Superstar**—Everything plus PM merchandise, free downloads, and 50% discount on all webstore purchases

For those who can't afford $30 or more a month, we have **Sustainer Rates** at $15, $10 and $5. Sustainers get a free PM Press T-shirt and a 50% discount on all purchases from our website.

Your Visa or Mastercard will be billed once a month, until you tell us to stop. Or until our efforts succeed in bringing the revolution around. Or the financial meltdown of Capital makes plastic redundant. Whichever comes first.